W9-BLT-570

"This is a wonderful book that can facilitate readers into being the person they've always dreamed of being! Through her own life examples, Jenny conveys great truths in a way that is virtually effortless to comprehend, and *A Short Path To Change* is packed with viable tools to empower each reader's transformation into experiencing more of the Divine Essence that we truly are."

—James A Sinclair, Award-winning
Filmmaker of *The Grand Self*

"Jennifer Mannion has written a manual for awakening consciousness. This book is a bridge for those looking to wake up into a new dream. It is essential reading for those who need to know there is much more to life and the new realities that await them."

—Alan Steinfeld, Founder of New Realities Media

"As we find ourselves in a transformational time in our lives, we often look to others to provide a guide or roadmap into uncharted territory. What I have found with Jenny Mannion's book *A Short Path To Change* is one-stop shopping. When you are in a hurry to turn your life around, you don't have time to stop at several different stores. Jenny delivers proven techniques for opening your connection to who you really are, which allows you the find the fastest route to where you need to be."

—Michelle Walling, Staff Writer of In5d.com

"A combination of deep wisdom and practical application, *A Short Path to Change* offers a path to healing for those who read it. Jenny Mannion takes her own experience and translates it into something that will work for those who seek positive change in their own lives."

—Deborah Blake, Author of *Everyday Witchcraft*

"This is an excellent primer in discovering new ways of thought to improve your experience in this body in this lifetime … [and] it does it all in clear, simple-to-read language which stimulates the reader into wanting to explore the process for themselves."

—Andrea de Michaelis, Publisher of *Horizons Magazine*

"Change always seems daunting to the human mind. We are creatures of comfortable habit and refuse to change our ways simply because we think it's difficult. But Jenny's book kicks all those difficult ways to change out the window and gives you simple, clear, wise and doable ways to create positive change within you. Jenny's journey is inspiring and learning from her life's work has been a blessing for me. I recommend this book to everyone who really really wants to create positive change within themselves and add happiness to their life. A must read!"

—Zeenat Merchant Syal, Counseling Psychologist, Spiritual Counselor, Naturopath, Holistic Healer, and Founder of PositiveProvocations.com

a
SHORT
PATH
to
CHANGE

About the Author

Jenny Mannion graduated from Penn State University with a BA in psychology and has always been interested in how the mind works and in helping others. She began her own transformation by healing herself of several chronic dis-eases in three weeks. Since healing, Jenny has become an alternative healing practitioner, mind/body mentor, and inspires people to connect with their inner power to create the life they desire. Jenny has witnessed clients in her own practice heal from depression, cancer, MS, and many other chronic dis-eases, becoming not only healthy but creating a life they always dreamed of. It is Jenny's passion to help others tap into their own inner powers to transform their lives. Jenny is originally from New York City and now lives in upstate New York with her two children.

Author photo © James R. Mcilroy www.jamesmcilroy.com

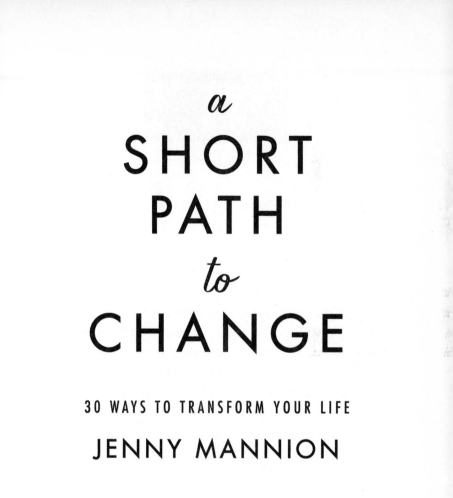

a SHORT PATH *to* CHANGE

30 WAYS TO TRANSFORM YOUR LIFE

JENNY MANNION

Llewellyn Publications
Woodbury, Minnesota

A Short Path to Change: 30 Ways to Transform Your Life © 2016 by Jenny Mannion. All rights reserved. No part of this book may be used or reproduced in any manner whatsoever, including Internet usage, without written permission from Llewellyn Publications, except in the case of brief quotations embodied in critical articles and reviews.

FIRST EDITION
First Printing, 2016

Cover art: iStockphoto.com/38920536/©bgblue
            iStockphoto.com/37063934/©NI QIN
Cover design: Ellen Lawson
Editing: Rosemary Wallner
Interior illustration: Mary Ann Zapalac

Llewellyn Publications is a registered trademark of Llewellyn Worldwide Ltd.

Library of Congress Cataloging-in-Publication Data
Mannion, Jenny, 1969–
 A short path to change : 30 ways to transform your life / by Jenny
Mannion. — FIRST EDITION.
    pages cm
 Includes bibliographical references and index.
 ISBN 978-0-7387-4561-9
1. Change (Psychology) 2. Chakras. 3. Emotions. 4. Thought and
thinking. I. Title.
 BF637.C4M325 2016
 158—dc23
                        2015015272

Llewellyn Worldwide Ltd. does not participate in, endorse, or have any authority or responsibility concerning private business transactions between our authors and the public.

 All mail addressed to the author is forwarded but the publisher cannot, unless specifically instructed by the author, give out an address or phone number.

 Any Internet references contained in this work are current at publication time, but the publisher cannot guarantee that a specific location will continue to be maintained. Please refer to the publisher's website for links to authors' websites and other sources.

Llewellyn Publications
A Division of Llewellyn Worldwide Ltd.
2143 Wooddale Drive
Woodbury, MN 55125-2989
www.llewellyn.com

Printed in the United States of America

Contents

Section IV: Discovering New Ways of Thought and Tools to Help

The material provided in this book is not a substitute for professional medical or therapeutic advice. Do not discontinue current medical or other treatment unless advised by your healthcare professional. The publisher and author make no promise that your situation will be remedied if you follow the information provided in this book.

Acknowledgments

I want to thank my mother, who is my inspiration of unconditional love and patience as well as one of my dearest friends. I would like to thank my father for teaching me to read when I was two years old and encouraging my thirst for knowledge. Thank you to my two wonderful children, Alex and Christina, who are a never-ending source of learning and love and make me smile; I'm so very proud to be their mom.

I would like to thank all my friends and soul family (you know who you are). Patricia Virasi, Justin Deichman, Angela Deleski, and Leslie Parmerter, in particular, you all helped me through my toughest life transitions. Without you I would not be who I am or where I am right now. And a huge heartfelt thank you to Vincent Garufi. Vinny, your love and support let me know I could accomplish finishing this book. You enrich my life in countless ways, Vinny, and I am so very grateful for you in my life each and every day!

Thank you so much to all the people involved in this book writing process. My incredible editor, James Spinella, whose advice was priceless and who I could not have completed this book without. Thank you to author Marilou Trask-Curtain, who encouraged me to submit my book to my wonderful publishing company, Llewellyn. Thank you to Llewellyn for this opportunity. Amy Glaser, thank you for your patience with me in my learning process!

INTRODUCTION

"Our deepest fear is not that we are inadequate. Our deepest fear is that we are powerful beyond measure. It is our light, not our darkness that most frightens us. We ask ourselves, 'Who am I to be brilliant, gorgeous, talented, fabulous?' Actually, who are you not to be? You are a child of God. Your playing small does not serve the world."

—MARIANNE WILLIAMSON

It has been such an honor and passion to write this book as well as a continuation in my own journey to healing and health. About eight years ago, I overcame more than six years of chronic disease and pain. I had been diagnosed with such illnesses as chronic mono, Factor V Leiden (a genetic blood disorder), fibromyalgia, and benign hypermobility syndrome (Ehlers-Danlos syndrome, type III). After healing myself of all of these illnesses in about three weeks and getting myself off of all medications within a year, I came to the profound realization that we are indeed more powerful than we were ever told. Instead of being in a wheelchair and never dancing again as my doctors had predicted, I became healthier than I had been in twenty years and even joined a belly dance troupe for a couple of years.

My passion for learning about the mind-body connection and helping others to do the same was ignited from my past healing experiences and has only grown in power and intensity over the last seven years. This passion has led me to become an alternative healing practitioner helping people all over the world come into their own power of self-healing. I have a never-ending passion for learning more and have given workshops and helped hundreds of clients.

Writing this book felt like a good vehicle to reach more people. I know people can change quickly because I healed myself in twenty-one days and had no guidance except my own intuition (and the wonderful authors and teachers I came across). In this book, I have pulled from my own learning experiences, the numerous resources and knowledge I have accumulated, as well as the many blocks and patterns I have encountered in working with clients.

The purpose of this book is to help you discover your own inner power for healing aspects of your own life. Remember, we are all self-healing creatures. We get a cut and it heals because we know it will. Doctors and society do not tell us to worry about it and that it will fester and get worse. There are many aspects of our past programming and life thus far that affect our healing capacities and energy. If we have buried emotions or events that we have not dealt with or if we have fallen into patterns of behaviors that do not suit us, our emotional and physical health will suffer. This book will teach you how to get in touch with unveiling some of these trapped emotions and patterns and give you many useful tools to transcend them. While a total physical healing cannot be guaranteed, I can say that if you go through these thirty exercises, parts of your life and the challenges and patterns you previously experienced in them will be transformed.

We are all beings of unlimited potential. We have not been told as much, however, but have been programmed from the womb with thoughts, emotions, and ideas coming from our parents, family, community, and collective consciousness. Many of us have heard of feats of extreme strength and healing that defy the natural laws; for example, the mother who finds the strength to pull a car off of her child or a late-stage cancer patient whose cancer disappears in an instant. We are quick to dismiss these events and think, "that person must be special." Well, we all are special. Each of us can tap into our unlimited power and special gifts, but first we need to connect to our inner self and rid ourselves of some of the previous programming. We need to connect with our energy body and chakra system and understand the messages our body constantly sends us. We need to fall in love with ourselves and, instead of berating ourselves, become our own best friend! We need to connect with our Higher Self and convince ourselves and see proof to truly believe we are unlimited and that anything is possible.

The thirty exercises in this book are in four sections and will teach you how to awaken to your full power and transform you into a person who confidently accepts his or her unlimited potential. This will put you firmly on your path to transforming many aspects of your life.

The book will be most useful if you start with Section I, Getting Rid of the Old Stuff—Internal Housecleaning, and then progress through Section II, Connecting with the Chakra System to Balance Your Energy Body; Section III, Staying in the Present Moment; and Section IV, Discovering New Ways of Thought and Tools to Help. We need to rid ourselves of the old stuff in order to be open to putting new patterns, beliefs, and behaviors in place.

Within each section, however, you can go through the chapters and their exercise in any order that speaks to you, though some chapters will refer to ones preceding them. Each chapter addresses something different, and you may be called to a chapter in particular to start with and I want you to honor your intuition.

I ask that you start with the intention to look at this book every day until you are done with all thirty exercises. Some exercises you might do in one day and feel ready to move on to the next one. For others, you may feel that you need to spend a few days on them. If you miss a day or an exercise takes you longer than a day, please do not be judgmental with yourself. Continue the exercises at a pace that feels comfortable and do-able so you will reach completion. Part of this journey is about trusting your intuition and that begins with the way you progress through this book. With some exercises, you will feel guided to do them more than once, and that is completely fine. Please don't rush yourself through. Each exercise is meant to be experienced fully. Have a notebook at hand, a computer file open, or paper available, as some exercises call for reflection through the process of writing.

Some exercises help to rid you of past programming and encourage you to look at things differently. Others enable you to understand the messages your body sends you, allowing you to tap into your energy body and balance your chakras. I offer you tools on how to stay present and share with you some of the most important things to remember as you step into this new space of power. Other exercises directly relate to finding and tapping into that power within. Some will resonate deeply, and you will carry them forward. A few might resonate so deeply, they will become something you practice regularly. Some you will do only once and know you are done. The ones that bring up resistance are usually the exercises that need to be done a few times. When we hit on something that is uncomfortable for us, our ego rises up, causes distractions, and tells us why we can move on and not deal with the current emotions (see "That Darn Ego—Moving Past the Resistance to Change" in Section I). It is important to recognize this tactic and remember to be kind to yourself if and when this comes up. I assure you this is a natural part of the healing process. If you truly feel you are not ready, make a note of the exercise and wait a few days or weeks before trying again.

Please donate at least a half hour per sitting for reading and completing each exercise. Some exercises can be done in five to ten minutes. However, in claiming that time and not rushing through the exercise, you give yourself permission to let these exercises fully integrate and change your life. Know that by getting through some of the challenging old stuff, you clear it out to make room for new patterns and behaviors. You experience the new you, which is actually the oldest you (your soul), and a new sense of power and peace will emerge.

As I mentioned, I cannot personally guarantee all dis-ease will disappear as it did with me. I will say these are powerful exercises, some of which I have seen help to transform and heal a good number of my clients. By committing to these thirty exercises, you send a powerful message to your Higher Self that you are ready for change. That message will go a long way to help shift patterns and behaviors in your life, and some will experience healing on all levels.

We all have unlimited potential, and it is my absolute pleasure to bring you this book and these exercises to tap in to it. Strap in and get ready for your short path to change. I feel with all my heart that if you do these exercises consciously and progress through all thirty, your life will truly never be the same!

SECTION I
Getting Rid of the Old Stuff— Internal Housecleaning

"If you want something new, you have to stop doing something old."

—PETER F. DRUCKER

You must get rid of the old to make room for the new. An internal housecleaning is necessary. You are not the culmination of old patterns, thoughts, and beliefs. You can always choose a new way of being. In getting to know your soul, you will feel a deep connection, a deep love, unlimited power, and peace and flow. As you peel off these old layers, you will meet some resistance but will also feel freedoms and connection like you have never felt.

From when you are born until the age of five, you are in a hypersensitive state of receiving. Your "automatic programming" is formed. Many people still react from this programming, even though it might not be in alignment at all with what they now feel or want. By looking at some of the ways you talk about and react to yourself and others, you can do some inner work and find what you want to change. This may seem scary or challenging as you begin to see and hear some of the patterns that have been built into you as your "go-to" reactions for so long. Know that by paying attention to them, you do yourself a powerful service. You shed the old habits, beliefs, and patterns that are not you, while you make room for new habits to emerge that serve you well. Noticing these habits and patterns of beliefs translates to freedom for you to truly be who you are. These habits and patterns might have been in place for the last ten, twenty, thirty, or even forty or more years, but as you will see, they don't take a fraction of that time to get rid of. Noticing them and being kind to yourself as you arrive at them is of critical importance. That is the first step toward healing and moving forward into your unlimited potential and creating a life more magical than your wildest dreams!

FORGIVENESS

"You must realize everyone is doing the best they can from their own state of consciousness."

—DEEPAK CHOPRA

Self-forgiveness and forgiveness of others is crucial in removing blocks so you can move forward to create the life you want. In my practice, I see lack of forgiveness as the number-one reason people cannot move forward, and it is the block that they cling to most tightly. There are different ways to look at forgiveness so you can shift the energy around yourself and your relationships with others. It might seem or feel very uncomfortable at first, but know that in taking this step, you let go of the past and make room for your future to be brighter and much more enjoyable.

Self-Forgiveness

Wow, are we hard on ourselves! Most of us are often our own worst enemies. We repeat phrases in our head such as "we should not have said, done, or even thought or felt" whatever we are criticizing ourselves over. Most of us would never speak to a loved one the way we speak to ourselves. We know instinctively we need to love ourselves more than anyone for our life to be in balance, but it does not come easy to us. We are not taught how to be kind, loving, and forgiving to ourselves. And this is not another thing to beat yourself up about! This is something you can learn now and in doing so, you can truly change the course of your life.

Forgiveness of Others

Please take a second to think about what forgiveness means to you. Sometimes saying the word to people can bring up very strong emotions. For me, forgiveness gives a feeling of freedom like no other. Whether it is self-forgiveness or the forgiveness of another person, this act grants us the permission and freedom to move on with our lives. Forgiveness doesn't have to mean you now love or approve of what occurred. It means you will no longer allow that incident, those words, or that inner dialogue of what happened hold you back. When you stay in a place of not forgiving yourself or others, you keep yourself rooted in that pain of the past. Even if you feel someone has wronged you, you still give them power over you by holding on to that anger, sadness, or state of un-forgiveness. Only in forgiving can you truly move forward and appreciate the current moment without being tethered to the past.

As the quote by Deepak Chopra acknowledges, "You must realize that everyone is doing the best they can from their own state of consciousness." When people "wrong" us or do something we perceive as bad, that usually means they are not happy with themselves. They act and react from the space they are in and what has been demonstrated to them and experienced in their own lives. They act out their own patterns. Most people, unless they are sociopaths, will not hurt another intentionally. If they hurt someone, it usually means that is something they have been shown and learned in their own life. An example would be an abused child who later in life grows up to abuse others.

Forgiveness can bring up some resistance, primarily due to the fact that you have become so attached to the emotions associated with whatever event you hold on to. Consequently, you sometimes might require a little help moving on to the step of forgiveness and will need to reframe it in your mind. You might wish for a way to do it where you would not be fighting the unstoppable voice inside your head, which frequently can repeat to you that you are not ready to let go of this perceived wrongdoing. The tool I have found most useful for this is Ho'oponopono (pronounced *Hoe-oh-pono-pono*), a Hawaiian prayer and form of healing. The name may be hard to say but the prayer is the easiest and most profound and powerful of all I have encountered. In saying this prayer, you can activate deep healing and forgiveness for yourself and for others.

Ho'oponopono

When I heard the case of Dr. Len using Ho'oponopono to release and heal his clients in a criminal psychiatric hospital, without even seeing them, I knew I had to know more. Dr. Len was a psychiatrist at a notoriously harsh criminal mental institution in Hawaii. Instead of seeing the clients for normal counseling sessions, he sat with their file for the allotted session time and said the Ho'oponopono prayer for them. Within a few months, people noticed a difference and patients were taken off of their medications. Violence was down, plants grew on the grounds where they never could before, and the whole attitude of the place changed. Within a few years, many of the patients were released. He had healed a huge percentage of the people in the hospital without even meeting with them!

Ho'oponopono is based on the fact that we are all connected and that we are a hundred percent responsible for the reality we create. As Dr. Len puts it, "Have you ever noticed that when you perceive a problem you feel like you are there?" Accepting that it is your responsibility does not mean it is your fault. It means you are responsible for healing yourself in order to heal whoever or whatever appears to be your problem.

This prayer works by truly talking to our soul and the souls of others. We are all connected at soul level. At soul level, there are no limits and we know we can always forgive and that we are responsible for what we create and for how we perceive reality. We are limitless, we can heal, and we are always capable of love. We can examine the negative feelings we have held so tightly and know we are strong enough at soul level to heal them. The Ho'oponopono prayer consists of four simple sentences, and I highly recommend you begin by using it for some self-healing and forgiveness. If you are like most people, you are often way too hard on yourself! However, if you were able to truly understand how perfect you are and that everything is a learning experience, you would always treat yourself with the same kindness you show your closest loved ones.

I recommend taking at least a few minutes to say this prayer, though even in saying it a few times, you will feel its power. Take a second to center yourself and to become aware of your surroundings. Notice your breath. Become present and repeat the following four sentences:

I love you.
I am sorry.
Please forgive me.
Thank you.

As you say this prayer, I ask you to recognize that your human aspect speaks directly to your soul. By saying these words, you affirm your love for your soul. You apologize for letting your mind and this three-dimensional world get the best of you and carrying you in to a state of unhappiness when, in reality, all is truly perfect. You ask for forgiveness because you know you want to be truly connected and are sorry you put your soul through this, but you also acknowledge that it is challenging to be human sometimes. You realize you are responsible for these thoughts and emotions. You are grateful and pay this debt of gratitude by saying thank you for this love and forgiveness that is always present and available to you.

It can be very emotional and powerful saying these few sentences; feel them when you say them. This works whether you say the words aloud or silently. (Although I have found that the times I have allowed myself to utter these words out loud were even more profoundly powerful.)

If you do this for even a few minutes each day, for yourself, you will see a profound change in your life. If you do this for another person, look at it in the same manner. Your soul is reaching out and forgiving their soul. Most times, when we are hurt, it was not an intentional act on the part of the offending individual. That person simply reacted and acted from what they know and their own state of consciousness. They have not intentionally gone out of their way to hurt you because of anything you are or have done. If you find it hard to forgive someone and let go of the pain on the third-dimensional level, try this exercise and see what happens.

A few years ago, I was working on a project and had someone assigned to help me from a company I needed to collaborate with. This man was not very professional. When we had 9 a.m. meetings, he would frequently show up reeking of alcohol. He also smelled of shampoo and his breath didn't smell, so I didn't get the feeling he was drinking in the morning. I believe he drank so much the night before (and probably most nights) that the alcohol was literally seeping through his skin. There were many delays in him meeting with my team. When he finally did show up, he had one simple task: bring the piece we needed for the project. When I arrived at the meeting place, I saw him outside with his car doors and trunk open and a mess all over; he appeared distraught. He said he had made these plans a month in advance, had traveled four hours to meet with us, and had forgotten the one thing he had to bring. Needless to say, I was not happy. I tried to hide my disappointment and kept thinking that if this man was drinking so much that he reeked of alcohol 24/7, he probably was not a very happy person. Instead of cursing him or complaining about him endlessly and adding to that negative energy, I decided I would try doing Ho'oponopono for him. Within 48 hours, he was transferred off my project. This is a small example. I have had several in my own life, and I have had clients tell me repeatedly about the miracles Ho'oponopono has brought in to their lives.

Exercise 1: Learning to Forgive Yourself and Others with Ho'oponopono

Find a quiet space. Allow yourself ten minutes for this exercise and five minutes after. Take some long, slow breaths and notice them ... do not judge your breath, just notice and become aware of it and let the in and out of your breath bring you to this present moment.

For the first five minutes, say these sentences of Ho'oponopono out loud (your human self says them to your inner self—your soul):

I love you.

I am sorry.

Please forgive me.

Thank you.

Notice how you feel as you say the words. Mean them, feel them!

For the second five minutes, say these words and direct them to a person in your life. It can be someone who you feel needs healing. It can be someone who you have had a challenging time with. Understand, as Deepak Chopra says, "Everyone is doing the best they can from their own state of consciousness." You are not excusing anything that has been done but are connecting with that person at soul level and moving beyond the illusion that you truly know all the factors in a given situation. You take into consideration that you too have been adding to the energy of that person being a challenging person or wrong in a situation by replaying that to the Universe every time you think about them. When you say sorry, you say you are sorry for contributing to that energy and also know that person has his or her own challenges. You look beyond what that person might have shown in this third-dimensional life, and you look to his or her soul, which is also perfect as yours is. Say the prayer for this person for five minutes, feeling it and noticing how you feel:

I love you.

I am sorry.

Please forgive me.

Thank you.

For the last five minutes, write in your journal or sit and reflect about how you felt saying Ho'oponopono each time. Think about how saying it for yourself and then for the other person is a different experience.

The beauty of Ho'oponopono is its simplicity. You can say this in the shower, before bed, in the morning—silently or out loud. You will see a difference in how you feel the more you say this prayer.

INFLUENCES

"You are the average of the five people you spend the most time with."

—JIM ROHN

We are energetic beings and what we choose to surround ourselves with affects us tremendously. Whether it is people in our lives who cause us to feel depleted of all our energy resources or the daily news that we feel we need to hear even though it holds much negativity. There is also the physical influence of where we spend the majority of our time as well as what we feed our body. Every choice regarding what we spend our focus on and give our energy to has a profound effect on our well-being, physically and emotionally. There are ways to take account for what you bring into your daily life. Once that is done, you can make conscious decisions to change to more positive influences.

Emotional Influences

Most people have had some family members or friends, in which after spending time with them, you can feel almost completely drained of your energy resources. That is because in many ways, some people are doing just that: draining you. Some have even used the phrase "energy vampire," and it can sure feel like that after you leave someone like this: like you literally have been sucked dry of your energy! This is especially true if you are someone who is caring, empathic, and sensitive to energy. You may attract these people to you because they see your light and know (consciously or unconsciously) that just by being around you they will feel better. You can limit time with people who zap your energy and set boundaries so that you know you are taking care of yourself and your own resources first. I am not suggesting that you cut everyone out of your life who you feel might be negative. As far as negative people go, there are three ways you can shift the energy around you:

1. Do the Ho'oponopono exercise listed in the previous chapter for them. This is a powerful prayer for shifting energy between you and another person. Realize that if someone zaps your energy, they are not in a positive space themselves. They react as best they can from the resources they have. Sending them love, as you do in Ho'oponopono, can create dramatic changes quickly.

2. Set boundaries! Sometimes you need to physically see and be in contact with the people in your life who carry this negativity with them. They could be coworkers or family members; you might even be cohabitating with them. Know your limits. Assess how you feel before and after being with the

person. Set limits to the time you are with them and make sure you do something positive for yourself before and after the time you spend with that person. This will help you to replenish your energy supply.

3. Reframe how you see the person. Often people reflect what we expect. You often hear couples complain about each other after they have been together awhile. They forget or lose sight of all the amazing and wonderful qualities and why they picked their partner in the first place. Instead, they focus on the few annoying habits they see that begin to blind them from the good. You call this to you when that is what you expect. Your friend/partner can feel that energy and react accordingly. By switching how you think of someone and thinking about the positive aspects of that person, you may be surprised how things can shift in your relationship.

The other aspects of emotional influences are media and what you listen to every day. Many find themselves repeating in their heads how horrible everything is in the world after watching the news. It is easy to get caught up in this since you have grown up with the majority of news being "bad." The first story on the nightly news is usually negative and the one with the greatest tragedy. It would make you feel very different if instead you turned on the news and heard of how many wonderful things were done that day for others. Unfortunately, that is not the case in most mass media. I am not saying that you should not be aware of what is going on in the world. But there are ways to receive this information that are more positive than the traditional TV, radio, and Internet sites. You can choose to listen to five-minute segments instead of hours of it daily, as I know some people do. Hearing how awful everything is and discussing, dwelling on, and worrying about it can make you feel badly and take your energy. If you choose to listen to mainstream news, you will hear mostly negative news. Here are a few sites I recommend for happy or more positive news:

Daily Good—News that Inspires: www.dailygood.org

The Happy News: www.thehappynews.com

New Earth Daily: newearthdaily.com

Positive News: www.positivenewsus.org

Huffington Post (Good News): www.huffingtonpost.com /good-news

Sunny Skyz: http://www.sunnyskyz.com/good-news

There are also many other emotional influences, including what you read (novels or newspapers), what you listen to (talk radio or music genres), and what you watch (movies or television). All of these things can affect your energy and are experiences to be mindful of. You don't have to watch only comedies or always listen to music that is upbeat and positive. But I ask you to be mindful of how these influences affect you. Take note of how you feel before and after and then readjust your choices accordingly. This brings to mind people who listen to sad music after a relationship breakup. Listening to that type of music when you are already sad sinks you deeper in to that depression and sadness. This is the norm as has been portrayed in many movies and experienced by many people I have talked to, but this is obviously not a way to feel better about the situation. Pay attention to what kind of music you listen to and what kind of mood you are in after listening. The same is true for watching television or movies. When we begin to pay attention and notice how these influences affect us, we can begin to make better educated decisions about what we want to surround ourselves with the majority of the time.

I love a variety of movies and television shows. I have noticed that the night's sleep I have if I have watched a scary or depressing movie before bed is different from when I watch a happy movie before bed. Scary or depressing movies also affect the way I feel when I wake up in the morning. I still watch sad or scary movies sometimes, but I try to choose comedic or light movies if I have had a long day or will be going to sleep soon. Beginning to notice is the first step toward making decisions that will help you feel better instead of making you feel more depleted.

Physical Influences

Internal Physical Influences

There are thousands of books written solely on our internal body and how to nourish it properly. You probably have heard the expression "you are what you eat." You certainly know that daily exercise of some kind rather than sitting on a couch all day is a more healthy option. Some people have struggled their whole life with these two issues and some have found as they get older it is more challenging to stay healthy. I am not here to lecture on food and exercise choices but to tell you to be mindful of what your body needs and asks for. It makes sense that what you feed yourself on all levels affects your energy makeup and how you feel on a daily basis. If you are only eating processed non-whole foods and not exercising, your body will be much weaker than if you feed it nourishing foods, drink water, and exercise.

I am not asking you to become vegan or start some extreme exercise regime. I am asking you to simply pay attention to your inner dialogue around these two areas of your life. Notice if you talk positively to yourself about the way you eat, your weight, and how much exercise you get. Or begin to notice if your habit is to insult yourself and tell yourself you are not good enough physically. It is very important to watch your inner dialogue around these issues as they help to shape your habits. Be easy but mindful of yourself as you explore this area. The more you become present and conscious, the healthier decisions you will make for yourself each and every day. We will explore this more in "Intention Setting—Mini Goals" in Section IV.

External Physical Influences

Your home is where you spend the majority of your time, and it is a powerful influence over your state of mind. You have probably heard the expression, "the home is your castle." When you think of an image of a castle you probably do not picture it cluttered with newspapers and stuff you need to maneuver around. Nope, there are open spaces that give a sense of airiness and flow. If your house is filled with clutter, it influences you negatively and creates a lack of flow. Even if you are not cognizant of it, when there is lack of room for energy to flow, it becomes stagnant. When you clear out what you don't need, you make room for the new. Where you spend the bulk of your time is an important part of how you feel. Donate clothes you no longer wear, throw out unused or broken items, clean house. It is so freeing when you reduce clutter, and it sends powerful messages to the Universe. You are grateful for all that you have and release what is not useful anymore!

~~~~~~~~~~~~~~~~~~~~~~~~~~~~~~~

Exercise 2: Taking Inventory and Assessing the Influences in Your Life

This exercise covers all the influences in your life discussed above: emotional, internal physical influences, and external physical influences.

Emotional Influences: I would like you to write a couple of lists. First, list a few people who, after you spend time with them, affect you in a negative way, decreasing your energy or resulting in irritation or worry. Then list a few activities (news watching, for instance) that result in that negativity. Next, list people who make you feel great after you spend time around them. List the activities you do that make you feel positive. Make this list total five things and/or people that make you feel positive. Think about practical ways you can start to decrease the time you spend surrounded by negative influences and increase the time with the positive influences. Put that plan into action today!

Emotional Influences, Optional: (If you have a spouse, friend, family member, boss, or coworker who has a habit that drives you crazy, this exercise is for you.) Think about some things you like about this person. When you know you will see them next, spend a few minutes beforehand concentrating on his or her positive aspects instead of that habit that drives you crazy. Get into a positive-feeling state before you meet the person. Write about what you encountered when you tried this and how the energy shifted. We will also get more into this in "Attention Shifting" later in this section.

Internal Physical Influences: Notice what words come to mind when you hear the words "diet" and "exercise." Are they positive or does this begin a running negative dialogue? I want you to affirm to yourself that you love yourself. Also affirm that as you work on transforming your life, you will want the best for yourself in all areas of your life. Pick one thing that you might like to see change that you know would make your body healthier. It could be eating more vegetables, drinking more water, exercising one time a week, etc., and write it down. Nothing too extreme right now—no daily exercise for three hours a day if you have not exercised in years; nothing that will cause a lot of resistance—just a small goal. Tell yourself this is a goal and you will be mindful of it and not insult yourself if you find yourself not doing it. This is a process and you are in the beginning of this process. Congratulate yourself for becoming cognizant of this desire to better yourself. Write down how it felt claiming this goal.

External Physical Influences: De-clutter one area where you spend a lot of time. If it is your bedroom, empty out a closet. If you want to tackle your office, get rid of unused papers. Maybe your living room can use some straightening or purging of magazines and newspapers or knick-knacks collecting dust. Many people have unused items in the kitchen that are disposable or can be sold at a yard sale or given to a consignment store. You will be amazed at how good it feels when an area is clean and clear!

Write down how you felt after doing each of the above-mentioned exercises. Did you feel relieved? Did you have more energy? This is something to keep active stock of through your life as your home situation and the people you attract in to your life begin to shift.

FEAR AND WORRY

"Nothing in life is to be feared, it is only to be understood. Now is the time to understand more, so that we may fear less."

—MARIE CURIE

Worry and fear are two negative emotions that do not support forward movement in your life. They keep you in the future and force you to put energy toward what you don't want. In recognizing your fears and what you are worried about, you can truly uncover what makes you tick. You can then work from there to infuse yourself with confidence instead.

There are so many acronyms for fear that describe it perfectly!

False (Evidence, Emotions, or Expectations) Appearing Real

Failure Expected And Received

Fighting Ego Against Reality

Forever Escaping And Retreating

Forgetting Everything is All Right

Frustration, Ego, Anxiety, Resentment

Future Events Already Ruined

None of those sound positive. Fear is always a barrier that will stop us from moving forward.

One of the best lessons I ever heard on fear came from Neale Donald Walsch in his book, *When Everything Changes, Change Everything* (EmNin Books, 2009). He explained that even fear is an expression of love. When you fear someone or something, you fear it because you love yourself and want to protect yourself or another person you love from that "thing." This helped me come to such a place of peace about fear. Knowing this and embracing that love, instead of the fear, allows you to examine the fear from a different perspective.

Most would agree that an abusive relationship (whether emotional or physical) is an extreme and valid example of fear. There is a fear of that other person because of our inherent self-love and want for safety and well-being coupled with the knowledge that the situation is not a healthy one. When you acknowledge that you love yourself enough to want what is good for you, you can begin to move past the state of being paralyzed in that fear. You can move to what you can do to change the situation, allowing yourself to move into a place of confidence and power. There are always organizations, friends, family members, community members, or people in groups that you can reach out to that have been in similar situations. There are ways to move yourself into that place of power instead of that place of fear that can literally immobilize you. There are also many ways to ask for help as you will learn about in "Community and Friends—Asking for Help" in Section IV.

The opposite of fear is love. When you allow yourself to find that space and understand where the fear comes from, you can begin to push past it, into a place of self-confidence. The more you trust yourself and your inner guidance and intuition, the more you can move forward with confidence. You will know you can feel better and that any fear or worry will only keep you from doing so.

When you worry, you actively put energy into what you don't want. Most people tend to worry about what someone else will say or what will happen if they react in a certain way. When you put as much energy into intending what you want, instead of worrying about what you don't want, it can put you in a much more hopeful state. It also says to the Universe you allow other possibilities. It is an easier switch to make than you might think. Once you look at what you tend to worry and have fear about, you can then ask yourself about other possibilities, including what you want to create, what is the best-case scenario, and what a miracle would look like in this situation.

I experienced this firsthand with my own physical health; I was overwhelmed with so much fear and worry. I was in my mid-thirties with two children to care for, and I felt helpless. I was told I would be in a wheelchair, possibly as soon as within a year. I was told I would be on painkillers my whole life and would have to begin physical therapy because the pain and conditions would get worse. With doctors I trusted telling me these so-called facts, there seemed to be no other possibility of any different outcome. But I saw my health totally change in three weeks by simply switching off the worry and fear and allowing for other possibilities. I know what worry and fear can do to you and how it can literally paralyze you. I also get to see what many would call "miracles" every day and see what happens when we allow ourselves to get past that fear and worry in my clients. You can create a better life for yourself. Limiting fear and worry is a powerful way to begin that journey.

~~~~~~~~~~~~~~~~~~~~~~~~~~~~~~~

Exercise 3: Pushing Past Fear and Worry

For this exercise, first list the top three things you worry or have fear about. It could be money, a failing relationship, a health problem, or your kids making the right decisions. There is no limit to what we can choose to worry about. For now, I want you to just list the top three that come up.

Next, list two positive outcomes for each. If it is money: maybe you will receive unexpected money from somewhere, maybe you will find money, or maybe someone who owes you money will pay you back. There are numerous positive scenarios. However, when you get deep in that state of worry or fear, sometimes there is a tendency to repeat how bad it is, not allowing for other possibilities. It might be helpful to think of what you would suggest if a friend was saying they were worried or fearful about something. Sometimes it is easier to come up with more solutions for other people than for yourself.

When you have those three things you are worried about, with two corresponding positive outcomes, sit with each for three minutes. Get into that emotional state of what if this positive scenario did work out and this was not a worry or fear anymore? The more you feel the emotions of a positive outcome, the more you bring it into the realm of possibility. Think of how many times you spent worrying or filling your head with negative messages. The amazing news is those were all past reactions, thoughts, fear, and worries coming from your subconscious. You now get to choose consciously what is possible and experience how good that will feel.

If you have the time, write down what it felt like when you allowed those positive possibilities into your reality. Did you feel relief? Excitement? Possibility? All of these are positive states that can help your fears transform into possibility.

NEGATIVE SELF-TALK

"The inner speech, your thoughts, can cause you to be rich or poor, loved or unloved, happy or unhappy, attractive or unattractive, powerful or weak."

—RALPH CHARELL

As humans, we can truly be our worst enemies. We allow ourselves to berate and belittle ourselves in a manner in which we wouldn't dream of doing to anyone else. We concentrate on the things done wrong, expressed inaccurately, or possibly all of the mistakes we feel we have made. It is unusual for us to give ourselves the proper recognition for things that we did right. We tend to concentrate on all the ways we screwed up. When we start to listen to our self-talk, it can be pretty scary and revealing as to why we feel the way we do about ourselves, why perhaps, we have such a negative self-image. In truly hearing and altering our self-talk, it can change our interior dialogue to a more constructive conversation that will empower us instead of disempower us.

On top of all the negative self-talk about ourselves, we usually are quite skilled at giving a negative running commentary of what is going on. We judge others and situations based on our past, sometimes not allowing for any new possibility. What we focus on expands. When we repeat these negative words we do not allow for any other scenario to present itself. In fact, we might actually block any other possibilities from coming into our lives. Where we put our energy helps to create our reality.

When I was sick, I kept telling myself I was sick as the doctors confirmed it every week with more and more tests. I did not allow my body to make healthy cells. The only thing I repeated to myself was just how sick I was and how badly I felt. I did not allow for any other possibility. The doctors told me I was ill and would deteriorate and I believed that in every cell of my body, which, again, did not allow healthy cells to be created. One of the main facts I learned that helped me to heal was that our body is 99.999 percent new every eleven months. It made sense to me that where our emotions are and what we tell ourselves are key. For years I had told myself I was sick. What if I began to tell myself that I was working on getting better? This worked and was part of the reason I healed myself in three weeks. It is so powerful to hear your inner dialogue and ask yourself if you truly believe what you are saying, where the best place for your energy is right now, and how you can reframe this?

The messages you send yourself may be deeply rooted. These messages can come from your family, community, or even global consciousness, and they developed into patterns early on in your life. You may have spent ten, twenty, thirty, or forty or more years repeating these same patterns. That being said, it is important that as you notice these statements, you are kind to yourself and give yourself a pat on the back for even noticing—even when you notice after the fact. It is a step, and each step is to be celebrated. It's just as if you had experienced what you considered a misstep, you would be sure to focus your attention on it. The great news? Even if it is a forty-year-old pattern, it will not take forty years to break it; in fact, it will not even take one year. When you focus your energy and attention on noticing, being present, and recognizing, you will be amazed at just how quickly you can change some of these patterns and messages.

An example is anything you have been critical of and have spoken of negatively to yourself. Perhaps you have told yourself you are not smart enough, good looking enough, or the right weight. Maybe you have replayed conversations in your head and have been judgmental about yourself and have told yourself that you wished you wouldn't have said or done this or that. When you insult yourself, you look at the past and what you have been up until this point, and judge. You negate the true you who is your soul and is love. You are not being kind to yourself and in doing so, are not attracting others to be kind to you. You limit yourself, increase negativity, and make it challenging to be in a positive state. You make yourself a victim of your own mind.

We will delve in to self-love in Section III, as it is an important concept and a state we are not used to acknowledging. We are taught to treat others as we want to be treated; unfortunately, we are not taught to treat ourselves as we would want to be treated. It begins with us and how we see and communicate to ourselves. Noticing is the first and most important step.

I had a challenging time when I began listening to my negative self-talk. I could not believe how hard I was on myself. It started to make a lot of sense as to why I felt weak, limited, and a victim of life. Remember, this is a step to empower you. In noticing, you can begin to take action and make some changes that will instantly have you feeling better and more aligned with your soul.

~~~~~~~~~~~~~~~~~~~~~~~~~

Exercise 4: Becoming Aware of and Changing Your Self-Talk

Here are two different exercises, and I want you to pick the one that resonates more with you—or do both if you like.

Mental Exercise: Pay attention the next time you find yourself tensed up as a result of your inner dialogue. Be aware of what you say to yourself and about yourself. Take some time and notice, today or tomorrow, one or two situations that arise. Think about if this is something you truly even believe, or is it something you heard from someone else or believe because of a limiting belief from collective consciousness? If you notice after the fact, ask yourself how you could have changed that inner dialogue to feel better instead of worse. If you notice as it is happening, applaud! In that moment, give yourself huge credit and gratitude for noticing. Then find a way to change the energy of that moment. You can try reversing the statement and see how that feels.

Physical Exercise: I am not one for pain but during the beginning stages of noticing my self-talk, I did use the Rubber Band technique. For this technique, put a rubber band around your wrist and give it a snap when you find yourself berating yourself or others, or you find yourself in a state of negatively judging the situation around you. Nothing like a little negative reinforcement to make you stop a habit fast. Of course, this also is more effective if you follow it up with the positive mental exercise. Contemplate how you can switch it up the next time when you are in that space of negative self-talk.

The most important thing is to be kind to yourself when and as you notice. We are human. Most often, we have unfortunately been taught to concentrate on the bad. We are usually not taught how wonderful and powerful we are. It is rarely shown to us how to love ourselves. Being present and noticing your self-talk are huge in changing the way you see life, your energy, and what you are putting out there into the Universe. The Universe has no choice but to respond with the same kindness you show yourself.

ATTENTION SHIFTING

"When you change the way you look at things—the things you look at change."

—DR. WAYNE DYER

This one quote alone helped me tremendously in the process of healing myself. We choose what to see. Often we react from some state of previously held beliefs and patterns and do not act consciously at all. When you begin to realize where you put your energy and the perspective in which you view a situation, you can begin to decide if it is accurate and if there is a better place to put your energy. You can truly turn a few minutes of what would have been a negative spiral, into one of the happiest moments of your day, just by shifting your attention.

When I was ill, I felt like I had the flu most days. This lasted for more than six years. There were times when my body ached so badly that all I knew how to do was focus on it. When I decided that I could feel better than I had been, I focused all my energy on a little finger, a toe, or any single part of my body that did not hurt. I paid gratitude for that part of my body. I told myself that if that one part was healthy, then there were healthy cells in my body, and I was not as sick as my doctors said. I wouldn't say I felt a hundred percent better instantaneously, but I felt a lot better than I did during those many months of lying there, thinking about how badly I felt.

What you focus on truly does expand, and it is of the utmost importance that you begin to realize where your attention goes. An example is when you wake up and something happens to make you think that this is going to be "one of those days." Maybe you overslept, spilled coffee, or stubbed your toe running around and getting ready for the day. This one thing has happened and already you put your attention on the one thing that went wrong. That sets the intention for more things to go wrong by labeling it as "one of those days." Instead, you could choose to laugh it off and think that what just happened really stunk but it's not the end of the world. You could also possibly change the pattern you were creating and declare that you are ready for this day to be a great one. You have the ability to switch your attention to create a more desirable outcome, but the first step is becoming aware of where your attention goes.

Imagine yourself in a grocery line. Yes, you need to do things after this but nothing life threatening will happen if you are ten minutes later than you anticipated. The person in front of you is having trouble at the register—maybe an item needs to be price checked or their account needs attention. Whatever the hold up is you know it will be a while. Can you now imagine what your initial reaction usually is? Some of the most common reactions to this situation are sighing, rolling your eyes at the person behind you, fidgeting and checking your phone, or getting anxious about these few minutes that are now ruining your day. What if, in that moment, you decided to give the person in front of you or the checkout person a kind smile? They probably are not feeling too great and could benefit from some positive energy being sent their way. You could decide to show amazing awareness of that moment and do something positive, instead of putting out negative energy. You could take a moment to think of things you were grateful for. You could take some breaths and close your eyes. You could even strike up a conversation with someone in line and possibly brighten the moment for that person as well. You could also simply stand there in the understanding that there is a reason for you getting these few moments to yourself. Perhaps it is a gift and not something to ruin your day. Maybe this moment was to make you slow down. In shifting that attention, you can change the rest of your day and maybe the days of the people around you as well. We can decide in each moment how we are going to react. It is in noticing where your attention is focused, being present, and claiming that moment, that you truly gain power to change your reality. There is priceless power in having that awareness and choosing to shift your attention.

Attention shifting is also useful in relationships. So many times when you first get involved with someone—whether it is a significant other or a friend, boss, or coworker—you can think that person is near perfect. As you learn more about the other person, you may focus on an annoying habit or two. Sometimes that habit gets to be all you can see, and you cringe even seeing that person because you are waiting for it to happen. When it occurs, you wish you could disappear because of feeling so tense and annoyed. You can even put the energy out before you see the person. Say you dislike that your significant other chews with their mouth open. You may find yourself dreading dinner while you cook, obsessing over that, rather than the possibility of the conversation you will have and how nice it will be to sit down and discuss the day. Instead, you can think about something you love about that person. Perhaps, when they do that annoying thing, you can laugh to yourself about it, remembering how it drove you crazy but actually it wasn't such a big deal after all. Shifting your attention and energy allows for another possibility and for you to be in a much more positive frame of mind.

Exercise 5: Learning to Shift Your Attention to Change Your Current Reality

For this exercise, think of something that usually gets you stressed out; something that is a real trigger for you. It can be a person, a habit, or a slow driver ahead of you. Before that next moment hits, think about how you could shift your attention in that moment to something else.

For example, maybe you get stressed when you drive behind slow drivers. Promise yourself that the next time you are behind one, you will blast your favorite song and sing along as loud as you can. Or you will run through the list of things you are grateful for that day. You can do anything but concentrate all your stress on the fact that you are moving slower than you want to and worrying about being late. Maybe you have to work with a person who has an annoying habit. Try to imagine the best thing you can about that person. The next time they display that habit, picture that best quality instead of focusing on what annoys you.

When you do this, note how you feel and write down how it made you feel differently. Be sure to give yourself lots of gratitude for noticing how you felt in that moment!

ROLES VS. SOUL

"The soul that is within me no man can degrade."
—FREDERICK DOUGLASS

When I ask the question, "Who are you?" what comes to mind? Do you think about a list of the roles you play in this lifetime: mother, father, daughter, son, husband, wife, brother, sister, friend, or your job description? We are not the roles we play, yet we identify with them so much sometimes that we lose sight of who we really are. We are not even the culmination of things we have told ourselves about who we are—we are, in fact, much deeper than that.

We are our soul, or Higher Self, which this book will help you to connect with. We are this conscious being that is always connected to deep wisdom and love. By shedding these roles and limitations, you peel off layers of restrictions. As you peel off these layers of roles or past beliefs, you will have more and more moments of connecting with your soul, the true you, and you will begin to fully appreciate all the gifts and opportunities that offers. Connecting with your soul and discarding the roles allows you to get more in touch with what truly fills your heart with joy, love, and passion. The more you become in touch with your soul and the more you do not allow roles to define you, the more life can flow with simplicity and grace. In listening and getting to know the true you, your soul, you become empowered and limitless.

I remember being an at-home mom for a few years and feeling like I had no idea who I was. Yes, I was a mom and loved being one. I was a wife and daughter and a friend to many. But who was I? I explored some of my passions to try and get in touch with that answer; I even found a few. I loved trance (yoga dance) and had always had dance in my life, I loved reading and helping friends however I could. But the truth of who I was wouldn't come until years later, during my process of healing.

One of the issues with only identifying yourself with roles is the judgment that comes with it. You may ask yourself and constantly judge yourself on if you are being a good parent, supportive enough friend, a caring and helpful enough child to your aging parents, doing a good enough job at work, and so on. It is natural to also hold many ideas and beliefs from collective consciousness and from the environment where you grew up. Your family / tribe also suggests and holds judgments on what it means to be in each of these roles. It becomes yet another thing to judge yourself on and to beat yourself up for. It also becomes limiting as you are not tapping into the true essence of who you are at soul level and what makes you truly you. In living from your soul, you will find life can be in flow and you can indeed live in joy. When you live from only the roles you play, you can find yourself feeling overwhelmed, stuck, and even resentful.

Your soul is the part of you that loves you unconditionally. Your soul is your essence, that is love, and it supports you living life in a state of love, joy, and passion. Your soul can whisper words of intuition and support and guide you into a state of flow like you have never known. You might wonder how you access this soul and know what or who that even is. You always have that access. Sections III and IV discuss living from your soul, and I offer many tools and exercises to do just that. For now, I want you to acknowledge it. You are more than your body and much more than the roles you have adopted or signed up for. You have so much more depth and love to you than you ever imagined.

Exercise 6: Moving Past the Roles to Get in Touch with Your Higher Self/Soul

Answer the question I posed, "Who are you?" Just allow yourself to write for a minute and see what quickly comes to mind. Notice if what you wrote is mostly roles.

Now, I would like you to answer the question, "What do you do that brings you joy?" This can be anything from laughing with friends, to singing, to going for walks. You can write about anything that you know will cause a smile to take over your face and will fill you with a sense of gratitude for that given moment.

Next, sit for a few minutes and feel the emotions of both of these questions. Spend a few more minutes on the second question, basking in what brings you joy and pleasure. When you get in touch with what brings you to life, you touch your soul. Ask yourself how can you bring more of those things in to your life, and affirm you are indeed bringing more of those things in to your life. Acknowledge the fact that you are so much more than the roles you play and that you are ready to know your soul intimately and live life from that space.

THAT DARN EGO
Moving Past the Resistance to Change

"If you want to reach a state of bliss, then go beyond your ego and the internal dialogue. Make a decision to relinquish the need to control, the need to be approved, and the need to judge. Those are the three things the ego is doing all the time. It's very important to be aware of them every time they come up."

—DEEPAK CHOPRA

Change can feel uncomfortable, challenging, and near impossible to our ego. It doesn't matter if what we move past is something that has served us or something that has been causing us heartache for years. When we know there is something we must change, we may begin to take steps to do that. But even if the Universe is providing us with resources to do it, simultaneously the ego can be at work telling us it is okay to stay right where we are. The ego gives us reasons why change isn't possible, causes resistance, and even causes us to self-sabotage. I look at it like a rubber band in a slingshot being pulled back farther and farther, building more and more resistance. In order for that rubber band to be released and us to be catapulted into that next stage of existence, we must let go and trust. I know, it is easier said than done in most cases, but there are ways to give our body, mind, and spirit the permission and the excitement to do just that.

I have heard the acronym "Edging God Out" for *ego* and whether you believe in God or not, living by following your ego is not the same as living from your soul and potential. Living from our ego separates us, makes us feel alone and disconnected from the Universe and everyone in it. It makes sense that if we feel alone, we feel the need to control, judge, and to be approved of. The ego can cause competition, feeling the need to prove oneself and look at life from a very close-minded perspective. You might be curious to know why we even have the ego. The ego serves to protect us from the unknown. However, as we evolve, we realize the unknown and what is beyond our body is what truly connects us all.

How do you know if it is your ego or Higher Self speaking to you? One good way to determine if it is the ego speaking, is the ego wants everything planned out and tells you it knows how it will all work out. Your soul is more in flow and knows that things come up every single day that influence your path and that you should take that next step first. Being in allowance and trusting that you are being shown the path as it unfolds is a good way to know you are tuning into your Higher Self. I am not saying that you should not make some long-term goals. But as I have seen time and time again, the more you hang on to only one way that it needs to be, the more the Universe will show otherwise. Your ego is in a hurry and feels the need to control, whereas your soul knows everything unfolds in perfect timing and continues to trust. If you feel hurried or rushed, that is the ego; your soul does not have a timetable. The ego believes time is limited, whereas the soul knows everything unfolds at the perfect pace and in Divine timing for your Highest Good.

Throughout the remainder of this book, I provide tools so you can better tune into your soul and know when it is speaking with you versus the ego. The more you quiet your mind and the third-dimensional world around you, the more you turn up the volume for your Higher Self to send you messages. In getting quiet and tuning in, you can ask questions and receive answers. You can also have faith and begin to trust that you are being led. This, in turn, allows you to let go of some of the control you were taught you need so that you can truly be led by your soul's guidance system. I view the chakra system as our body's physical diagnostic system, which is why that section is next. In tuning into your energy body, you can hear messages that the ego ignored or negated. There is great power in truly beginning to hear. In that power, you can form a trust that will allow you to move past that resistance to change and into the next phase of your life with joy and ease.

Exercise 7: Accessing the Unlimited Nature of Your Soul to Quiet the Ego

I want you to sit for a few minutes and get quiet. I will give you more ways to do that in future chapters. For now, just do the best you can to get in a comfortable, straight-back position, and close your eyes. You can watch your breath if that helps, but do not change or judge it—just notice it. If it helps, you may also begin to count your in and out breaths.

When you feel you are in a relatively calm place, do the following. First, imagine what your life would look like in three years if everything was perfect. There are no restrictions here, pretend you had enough money and resources to fulfill your deepest desires (if it helps, imagine this money just appeared in some unforeseen way).

Next, think about the people who are close to you, the home you live in, the car you drive, and what you do for a living. Imagine how much you make a year; if you are celebrating an occasion, imagine who is around you; think about where you go on vacation.

Now bring in every sense possible. Think about what your house smells like and looks like, what it feels like when you hear the joy of the people around you, what it feels like emotionally and physically to be in this space. The more you bring your emotions and senses into this vision the more real it feels and the more you call it to yourself as real, not simply a possibility, but a probability that it will occur. Smile during this exercise and if you feel any restricting thoughts come to mind, let them go and refocus on aspects of what you want to create. Give yourself a few minutes in this space. The more you do this exercise, the more you allow your soul to open up to the unlimited potential that is always available to us.

Many famous people have come from nothing to create the life of their dreams, and that can also be you! Billionaire Oprah Winfrey was born to unwed teenaged parents and ran away at the age of thirteen after being molested. J. K. Rowling, author of the Harry Potter books, had a mother who died early. She lived on welfare and suffered from periods of depression. Actor Jim Carrey worked eight hours a day in a factory during high school as he tried to assist his poor family. He had to drop out of school and live in a camper.

There is no reason except for the reasons the ego comes up with to make you believe you are limited, which as you know by now is simply not true. The more you embrace the unlimited potential, the more you silence the ego and decide you will not let it hold you back. You deserve it all!

SECTION I
CONSIDERATIONS

Did some of the exercises in Section I bring you to places that seemed very uncomfortable? Were you able to catch yourself in some habits that seemed less than positive? What was your reaction when you caught yourself? It is important to remember that this is a process. You are working on un-doing what has become comfortable to you. No matter how truly uncomfortable these patterns make you feel inside, there is a part of you struggling to hang on. See if you can smile at that part of you when it comes up. I try (and sometimes I am more successful than others) to laugh at myself if I see an unwanted pattern come up yet again. I have been known to internally whisper to myself, "silly human." The more you can make light about this journey and not pressure yourself to be there already, the more fun you will have with this whole process. Life is supposed to be fun and in flow; as you change these limiting patterns and behaviors, you tap into the part of you that is unlimited. The more you consciously tap into this part of you and alter these patterns, the more you will know and feel this power in every part of your body and soul. Be easy on yourself and enjoy the process. With the exercises that brought up some resistance, do them a few times, and be patient with yourself in the process.

Next I will teach you how to listen to your body's inner dialogue, which is always going on. Being aware of this inner dialog will help you on your Short Path to Change.

SECTION II
Connecting with the Chakra System to Balance Your Energy Body

"Chakras are energy-awareness centers. They are the revolving doors of creativity and communication between spirit and the world."

—MICHAEL J. TAMURA

Our body is always speaking to us. We experience this as we feel extreme emotions such as exhaustion and stress, but there are subtle messages as well. Practitioners of Eastern medicine look at the energy system as a way to diagnose and treat health issues. While Western medicine is very valuable, it excludes what I have found to be a priceless tool in finding out what is really going on with the body and more importantly, why. Our body gives us subtle clues when any of the chakras are unbalanced. By understanding the chakra system, we can better understand these clues and work with the energy body to balance it. The chakras can become unbalanced through any influence in our life whether physical or emotional. If we do not process emotions or a situation properly or we eat processed, non-healthy foods, the chakras can be affected and become out of balance. When energy is correctly flowing through our chakras and they are balanced, our organs can function properly and keep us in a proper state of health and well-being.

AN INTRODUCTION
TO THE CHAKRAS

"We aren't here to heal our illnesses; our illnesses are here to heal us."

—CARL JUNG

.

Understanding the chakra system is pretty easy in that it seems to just make sense the more you delve in to it. In this section, I offer a summary of each chakra, an outline of ways to understand what happens when one is over- or underactive, and an exercise to teach you how to balance each chakra. My goal is to simplify and demystify the chakra system so that it becomes second nature for you to incorporate in to your life and effectively balance your energy body.

So what exactly are chakras and where are they located? Chakras are part of our energy or subtle body. The chakras are seven major energy centers that can be described as wheels of energy spinning in each spot. This book discusses only these seven major chakras, although there are many more throughout the body and outside the body in our energy field. Chakras are the same colors as the rainbow beginning with the first "root" chakra, which is red, and ending with the seventh "crown" chakra, which is violet and located at the top of the head. When the chakras are in balance, life and emotions flow easily. When out of balance, you can feel discomfort or disease either emotionally or physically in different areas of your life. Learning about these can help you tune into your body's way of communicating to you what is out of balance and how to bring it back into a state of ease.

The chakras are your body's way of communicating when something is out of flow. These energy centers correspond to different parts of your body and different aspects of your life. Since healing myself, I rarely ever get sick. When I do show any symptoms of unwellness, I immediately go to my chakras to assess what in my life is causing this ache or imbalance. When I get a sore throat, I immediately know this is the fifth chakra speaking to me and is related to something I am probably not admitting to myself or communicating to others. Possibly, I am not hearing the truth of what someone is communicating to me. In recognizing the emotional issues surrounding my sore throat, and doing whatever is necessary to right that imbalance, I can cure the discomfort quickly, before it becomes a disease or serious ailment. For example, approaching what I have made up in my head as an uncomfortable conversation is usually never quite as bad as I imagined it to be; and by having that conversation, the physical pain can disappear. Even if it is a conversation that does turn out to have challenging consequences, it is still out in the open and not festering inside. There is a freedom to move forward with the physical symptoms gone.

I have written some descriptions and mantras for each chakra that explain them in simplistic terms. I also offer a short description of the key considerations of each. It is interesting to notice that the foods, flowers, and crystals that help balance each chakra are often the same color as that chakra. As you read about the chakras, you will notice how they seem to make sense and correlate with the parts of the body and emotions. Each chapter describes the physical and emotional challenges that are related to each chakra. At the end of each chapter is an exercise to balance the individual chakra. Each exercise is designed to allow you to feel that chakra and bring it in to balance; the charts at the end may make the exercises easier for you.

We are taught from a young age to run to the doctor when we exhibit any physical symptoms. While this may be appropriate in some situations (and I am not saying to never go to the doctor again), often before these symptoms become severe physical sensations, our body has tried to offer us clues that something was awry. We are usually too busy running through our day and distracted by technology and our to-do list so it never occurs to us to take some time, tune in, and ask our bodies on a regular basis if there is anything we need to do to keep it running properly. We know the common messages given to us for decades to eat right, exercise, and drink more water but it goes much deeper than that and includes monitoring and doing what is best to keep our subtle (energy body) in balance.

As mentioned in "Influences" in Section I, every single thing you allow yourself to be influenced by affects your well-being, whether you are cognizant of it or not. Some of these influences include relationships; messages you have heard continuously from your parents, community, or global consciousness; your physical surroundings; and every other possible interaction you have had in your life. It is up to you to recognize how your energy centers have been affected. You need to look at each and check in to see if these energy centers are in balance or if you are exhibiting symptoms of them being imbalanced. With this awareness, you can truly begin to understand how the outside world affects your health, and in many cases you can bring these energy centers into balance.

You might think you are not self-healing, but from the beginning you have been given signs that you are. When you get a scrape or cut, new skin will form and you will heal. It begins to get trickier if you come down with more severe symptoms; fear often sets in and you believe you need outside help to feel better. Sometimes that is the case, and again I am not saying to forgo seeing a doctor. I am saying that by being aware of these energy centers and checking in regularly, you can harness that power of self-healing and connectivity to the messages your body always sends.

An extreme case of how powerful belief is in altering our physical conditions is cited in my friend James Sinclair's movie, *What If?* He had heard of an inmate at a prison whose front teeth had been knocked out a few times and had always grown back. When the inmate was interviewed and asked how his front teeth grew back, he simply stated, "What do you mean? Teeth always grow back!" What you believe and tell your body about healing truly has an affect on your well-being. Learning about your energy centers is a wonderful way to see just how true that is and to begin to apply self-diagnosis and healing to your own life.

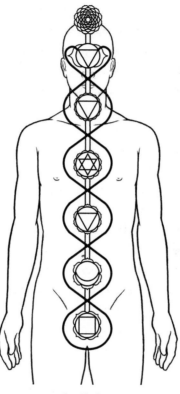

The Chakras

In the following chapters you will learn about the seven main chakras. They begin from the base of the spine (the first or root chakra) and end at the top of the head (the crown or seventh chakra).

This chapter includes a brief introduction about each chakra and an exercise to begin to become aware of each. The first three chakras are more about our human side; the last three, our more spiritual side; and the fourth, heart chakra, sitting right in the middle at our heart, connects those two worlds together.

The first "root" chakra houses beliefs we have been programmed with since birth and repeat daily even if they are not what we believe anymore.

The second "sacral" chakra is about creativity in all forms, meaning our creativity in our own lives. It also encompasses us being created, sexual relationships as well as male/female beliefs, relationships we have had, and how we create money and bring it into our lives.

The third "solar plexus" chakra is about our own personal power. It is the fire in our belly. It is courage and the willingness to step with integrity and self-confidence onto our path to success.

The fourth "heart" chakra is about the heart. It is about love and relationships and how we have processed emotions around them. It is about our ability to be open to love and relationships and to maintain and nurture the most important love relationship of our life: self-love with our inner being.

The fifth "throat" chakra is about communication, including speaking and hearing other people's truths. It is also about expressing ourselves through our creativity and ability to stand in our truth.

The sixth "third eye" chakra is all about intuition. It is about us being open to receiving guidance and tuning in to our specific way of receiving guidance and listening to our intuition.

The seventh "crown" chakra connects us with all else. It is about being connected to everyone else, the food we eat, and receiving Divine Wisdom.

These are basic descriptions and in the following seven chapters you will get to know each chakra individually well. For now, I want you to have a feel for them in general and the following exercise will help you connect with each.

Exercise 8: Discovering and Journeying through Each Chakra

This meditative exercise will help you locate and feel your chakras. Please read through the whole exercise ahead of time so you know what to expect and can relax in to it. You can also use the table after the exercise as an easy way to guide you through the steps.

I would like you to sit and take a couple of slow breaths to center and bring yourself to the current moment. Picture a white ball of energy beginning at your feet and working its way up your body. As it works its way up your chakra system, you will picture a color at each and say an affirmation for that chakra. You will then transmute that color back to white before moving it up to the next chakra.

The white light works its way up your legs and stops at the base of your spine, at your root chakra, where it glows red. As you see it glowing red, affirm to yourself, "I am protected and secure and have total faith that the Universe is constantly providing for me." Breathe into this statement and, if you like, repeat it a couple of times before picturing that red light transmuting to white light once again as it makes its way to your second, sacral, chakra and turns a bright orange.

Your sacral chakra is about two inches below and behind your naval. As you picture this orange light say the affirmation, "I am happy, secure in my physical body, passionate, and abundant." Again, breathe in a few times here if you want as you repeat the affirmation.

When you are ready to move on, transmute the light to white light and have it travel up to your third, solar plexus, chakra, which is at your upper abdomen in the stomach area as it turns to a bright yellow ball of light. Repeat the affirmation, "I am unlimited, I am positively empowered and am successful in all my ventures." Take those breaths again, repeating the affirmation and breathing while doing so.

When you are ready, transmute the light to white light and have it travel up to your fourth, heart, chakra. Here it glows green as you repeat the affirmation, "I am giving and receiving love unconditionally and effortlessly." Again, you can breathe here and repeat the mantra until you feel ready to transmute it to white light and move on.

The light now moves to your fifth, throat, chakra and glows blue. You repeat the affirmation, "I am expressing myself truthfully and clearly as I receive and hear other people's truths." Breathe and repeat a few times as you transmute that light again to pure white light.

The light then travels up to the sixth, third eye, chakra, in between your eyebrows and turns indigo. You repeat the affirmation, "I am connected to my intuition and am constantly receiving guidance." Repeat and breathe as you transmute the light to a white healing light.

This light now moves up to the seventh chakra at the crown of your head and glows violet. You repeat the affirmation, "I am present and connected to the wisdom the Universe always provides." Now one last time, after you say the affirmation as many times as you feel is needed, transmute that light to white light.

Now, picture that white light being sent up to the skies as it leaves your crown. Know that you have just tapped into the power of your chakras and what their true meanings and purposes are. Express gratitude to the Universe and to yourself for providing this service. Take a few deep breaths and write down how you felt after this exercise.

Exercise 8 Guiding Chart

Chakra	Color/Location	Affirmation
1st (Root)	Red—Base of Spine	I am protected and secure and have total faith that the Universe is constantly providing for me.
2nd (Sacral)	Orange—Two inches below naval	I am happy, secure in my physical body, passionate, and abundant.
3rd (Solar Plexus)	Yellow—Upper Abdominal Area	I am unlimited, I am positively empowered and am successful in all my ventures.
4th (Heart)	Green or Gold—Heart	I am giving and receiving love unconditionally and effortlessly.
5th (Throat)	Blue—Throat	I am expressing myself truthfully and clearly as I receive and hear other people's truths.
6th (Third Eye)	Indigo—In Between Eyebrows	I am connected to my intuition and am constantly receiving guidance.
7th (Crown)	Violet—Top of Head	I am present and connected to the wisdom the Universe always provides.

FIRST CHAKRA
The Root Chakra

"From my tribe I take nothing, I am the maker of my own fortune."

—TECUMSEH

Getting to Know the First "Base or Root" Chakra

When we are born we have our own body and soul but the world we come into heavily influences us. We receive messages from our "tribe" (family, community). We receive messages from the media and global consciousness. Even if we are not consciously aware of these messages, we take them in like a sponge until the age of five and these become part of our key belief programs. We can think of this first chakra as the one grounding us to Earth and our existence here. So everything created on Earth and how we believe (or don't believe) we belong here contributes to the health of this chakra.

Think about someone you know, or perhaps it could be yourself and your childhood. Both positive and negative messages directed at you affected how you saw yourself from a very young age. People who had a very challenging childhood, say with a parent who was emotionally abusive or absent, could have an unbalanced first chakra because they believe the messages they were told. People with an underactive first chakra can feel like they do not belong. They can feel weak, abandoned, unlovable, and insecure. When we begin to awaken and truly hear what we are telling ourselves (as we learned in "Negative Self-Talk" in Section I), we can start to ask ourselves if this is something we truly believe. Perhaps we are simply repeating these statements because we have been so used to hearing them in our own heads for so long. In noticing where these statements come from and using some of the tools such as Ho'oponopono for ourselves for holding this belief for so long, and for whoever this belief began with, we can truly begin to self-heal some of the wounds we have held in our first chakra possibly for decades.

If you feel unlovable, goals are hard to obtain. A person with an imbalanced first chakra can find it hard to move forward on Earth as they feel stuck in place.

If a person has an overactive first chakra, they can overcompensate for the beliefs that they are not good enough. They might be extremely judgmental of others and very self-involved. A person with excessive energy in the first chakra can be greedy, feeling the need to gain more to feel better about themselves. This is usually an overcompensation from their own past insecurities. Again, recognizing where these thoughts and beliefs came from, in a non-judgmental way, is the first step toward healing yourself from them.

The first chakra also represents that fight or flight instinct, which also makes sense. It is our ability to survive and feel comfortable on this planet and part of that is our instinct. The animals associated with this first chakra are snakes that survive on and in the ground. This chakra is all about the ground, grounding ourselves into this existence and the emotions we feel around doing just that.

When this chakra is unbalanced, we can look at the illnesses correlated with it and see how it makes sense: depression, because of not feeling totally comfortable in our own skin; arthritis or leg and bone issues because not feeling comfortable in our own skin translates into pain when we walk on this Earth; cancer, which is some of our cells attacking us and again, us feeling angry and unforgiving of ourselves or others. These are some of the reasons and results that can happen when the first chakra is out of balance. I am not discounting the physical triggers too, but for this description I am concentrating on the emotional triggers and what we can do to bring them into balance.

If the first chakra is balanced, we feel grounded, confident, courageous, and can have this joy of life here and know we can not just survive but thrive. Sometimes balancing the first chakra can seem a bit scary as it can definitely call for drudging up some not so pleasant memories. Know that any temporary discomfort is worth the joy you will feel once those beliefs are discovered and let go. You are not the culmination of negative thoughts and emotions that have been said to you, felt deeply, and repeated. You are an unlimited being looking to unearth whatever limits you have to face them head on and put them to rest.

Ways to bring this chakra into balance include grounding exercises such as walking, dancing, and certain yoga poses—feeling and honoring that connection to Earth. Taking B vitamins and drinking lots of water also helps your adrenals stay healthy and keeps this chakra in balance. Saying affirmations is also helpful, telling yourself what you believe that is positive about yourself. Recognize you are different from everyone else but also similar in many ways and celebrate your differences and similarities instead of allowing it to separate you. Forgiveness is also key to balancing this chakra, and Ho'oponopono is a great tool to achieve it. If you recognize that in freeing yourself of these negative emotions you can feel better about yourself and life in general, it becomes easier and not so challenging to accomplish. Holding on to negative emotions about yourself or others will only hold you in that limited space. Freeing negative emotions allows you to feel you belong and you deserve to be happy on this planet.

Notes on the First "Root" Chakra

Sanskrit Name: Muladhara

Location: Base of Spine

Element: Earth

Color: Red

Glands: Adrenal

Foods: Root vegetables such as potatoes, carrots, radishes, parsnips, onions, beets, garlic. Protein-rich food such as meats, beans, eggs, tofu, soy products, and peanut butter. Spices such as paprika, chives, and pepper.

Crystals: Red Carnelian (Balancing), Rhodochrosite (Clearing), Red Jasper (Activating), Black Tourmaline (Healing and Protection), Garnet (Balancing), Hematite (Grounding and Stabilizing), Smokey Quartz (Healing and Protection)

Flowers: Eucalyptus, Red Lily, Sundew (Drosera)

Yoga Poses: Uttanasana, Janu Sirsasana, Salamba Savasana, Salamba Balasana

Sound: Lam

Mantra: Om Gam Ganapataye Namaha

Affirmations for the First "Root" Chakra

I forgive and release the past and live in the present moment.

I am safe and secure at all times.

I am strong and I am able to handle any situation.

I take responsibility for who I am and how my life is.

The Universe is a safe place that always provides what I need.

I am thankful for all the opportunities for development and growth that have come my way.

I trust life supports me in fulfilling my purpose.

I love my body as it supports me on Earth.
I trust in the process of life.

Mental, Emotional, and Physical Aspects
of the First "Root" Chakra

Mental/Emotional: This is where we store the conscious and sub-conscious beliefs, from early in childhood, that we have received from our "tribe," be it our parents, community, global, or collective consciousness. The root chakra promotes physical survival, patience, courage, vitality, stability, and material success.

The first chakra will trigger a feeling of "safe" or "unsafe." This is where the fight or flight reflex comes from. Overconfidence or the other extreme of no self-esteem stems from this place as well. Also from this chakra are beliefs about wealth/abundance and savings; finances, having "enough," and your emotions about what that means for money, food, etc. An example would be someone who is a workaholic because "you have to" or if you self-sabotage and have a "victim" mentality. It also deals with our feelings of safety and security, our will to live, and our sense of being grounded and secure.

Physical (Body): The first chakra controls the adrenal glands, kidneys, spine, and the whole nervous system.

If the first chakra is not functioning correctly, it may lead to: obesity; arthritis; cancer; addictions; depression; sexual disorders; immune system issues; constipation; soreness or problems in bones, feet, legs, teeth, hips, and buttocks. It might also lead to anemia, fatigue, colds, bladder infection, leukemia. It can also lead to sciatica, varicose veins, rectal tumors/cancer, or auto-immune disorders.

~~~~~~

Exercise 9: Grounding and Healing with the First "Root" Chakra

Since you house all your limiting beliefs here, it is important that you take the necessary time to recognize some beliefs that have been limiting you, before beginning this exercise. These can be global statements you see yourself agreeing internally with; for example, "life is hard," "divorce is bad," "making money is difficult." I would like for you to come up with three limiting beliefs you have heard repeatedly. Focus on the limiting beliefs that at some level make you squirm enough to know that part of you (even if it is at a subconscious level) believes them. Please take a moment and write these down. Remember there is a chart at the end of this exercise to help you with it. Please read the whole exercise first before beginning.

You have already learned that core beliefs are formed from birth to the age of five. So, if at some point in that time frame you were told "you can't" or "this is bad," you will begin to believe it at some level. Whereas, a seed never doubts it can grow into a beautiful flower or a plant.

With these three "limiting beliefs in mind," I want you to take some deep breaths and close your eyes. Imagine a seed at the base of your spine where the root chakra is. Surround that seed with the red of heart love and say silently to your-self the opposite of those three beliefs. If a limiting belief is, "There is not enough money to go around." You will now say, "There is plenty of money to go around for everyone." Say each reverse statement three times. As you say each, take a breath and feel the truth of your new belief. As you speak each statement three times, imagine that seed sprouting and growing.

As you complete the second round of saying the second statement reversed three times, picture that seed growing strong and keep that red light on it. As you finish the third round, imagine the growth of the seed again. But now, see it flowering and imagine a lotus flower with four petals, which is the symbol for this chakra. It is healthy; you now have new beliefs taking the place of limiting ones. You feel stronger for it.

Please feel free to use this exercise as many times as you want, reversing as many limiting beliefs as you want. It is a good way to free yourself of thoughts and subconscious beliefs that no longer serve you. The chart below will help to simplify the exercise as you progress through it.

Exercise 9 Guiding Chart

Limiting Beliefs	Affirmation/New Belief	Process
1.	1.	1. Imagine a seed at the base of your spine (root chakra location) surrounded by red light. See the seed sprouting and grow-ing as you repeat the new belief.
2.	2.	2. See the seed grow-ing into a healthy plant as you keep the red light on it.
3.	3.	3. Imagine the plant has grown tall and a lotus flower with four petals opens and blooms strongly.
Repeat three times. As you breathe, feel the truth of each new statement.		

SECOND CHAKRA
The Sacral Chakra

"Happiness lies in the joy of achievement and the thrill of creative effort."

—FRANKLIN D. ROOSEVELT

Getting to Know the Second "Sacral" Chakra

"Creation" is the key word for the second chakra, and we create in many more ways than we were ever taught. Every relationship is a creation as are the boundaries we choose to set in them. We create our feelings and how we will react to them. We create our ideas about males and females and their roles and how that fits into our own lives. We create the feelings we have about money and how we will create and bring money into our lives. We create in the feelings we associate around food and sex and what we expect in intimate relationships. We also create when we procreate, bringing new life into this world. We create our patterns, and we can also begin to create the life we want once we are conscious and awakened to these patterns, beliefs, and emotions we have held on to.

The element of water is associated with this chakra, which makes so much sense because water is the base of all creation and it is what our bodies are mostly made of. It also makes sense that the organs associated with creation are affected when this chakra is not in balance. To bring this chakra into balance requires becoming conscious of the thoughts, emotions, and beliefs you have around everything you are creating in your life.

In my practice, I have noticed many people almost go into auto pilot mode with relationships. They will repeat the same patterns no matter how unhealthy they are because that is what they are used to. When you become conscious of what you want to create, it becomes a healthier place to begin a relationship for all parties involved. Of course there is the Golden Rule of treating people how you want to be treated. There is also setting boundaries and recognizing how the relationships in your life to this point have been healthy or unhealthy. You can begin to bring your current relationships into balance and set intentions for the new ones that you want to create. You need to be conscious of how you behave in relationships, noticing your own patterns and realizing what is working and what needs to be changed.

If you have been sexually abused or had any kind of intimate relationship that was unhealthy, it will need to be looked at to begin to heal and create new kinds of relationships. You will need to love yourself enough to know and claim that you want and deserve healthy relationships and do some inner work so that can be attainable. It makes sense that how you see yourself sexually also affects this chakra. Having a healthy body image and loving yourself as a sexual and masculine or feminine being in whatever form that means is important to this second chakra staying in balance.

If you grew up in an environment where expressing emotions was looked down upon, you might feel very resistant to change, have a fear of pleasure, or be detached from emotions as they come up. There is also the possibility of a drama-filled childhood, which also affects this chakra. Addiction can be common if this chakra is out of balance because there is that tendency to want to numb out instead of facing emotions. This can be done by taking drugs, drinking to excess, or overeating. It can also cause some to become overly emotional.

Taking stock of your emotions and feelings is key to this chakra. Recognize how you process emotions, honor and express them. When this chakra is not in flow and you do not process emotions or hold on to past patterns that do not serve you, many different physical ailments can arise. Dis-ease in the areas that this chakra is affiliated with include the hips, back, kidneys, and circulation. Fertility and dis-eases associated with sexual organs can occur.

There are many ways to bring this chakra into balance. Being around water helps as does beginning to face and deal with past issues around sex, sexuality, and boundaries in all relationships. Become conscious of your emotions as you have them and notice if they truly are your emotions. They could also be the emotions of someone around you, maybe a loved one, or they might be an automatic response that is not truly how you are feeling. Expressing your creativity however you see fit is also a wonderful way to bring this chakra into balance. Physically, eating orange foods or foods from water helps to balance this chakra.

With the second chakra in balance, healthy boundaries are set within relationships and you can process and express your emotions. You consciously create healthy relationships and are aware you are the creator of how you feel about everything in this life. With the second chakra balanced, it is easy to create in other forms, whether by cooking, writing, dancing, or however creation resonates with you. This chakra in balance aligns you with abundance, and bringing money into your life no longer feels like an effort but rather a flow. You have a healthy feeling of self-respect and a new strength knowing that you are in fact the creator of your life.

Notes on the Second "Sacral" Chakra

Sanskrit Name: Swadhisthan

Location: Between the pubic bone and the navel (lower abdomen)

Element: Water

Color: Orange

Glands: Endocrine gland, testes or ovaries, relates to lymphatic system

Foods: Fruits such as pears, watermelon, and bananas; honey; chocolate; bread and butter; dairy products, including milk, ice cream; wine, pastas.

Crystals: Orange Calcite (Activating and Cleansing), Orange Carnelian (Healing), Orange Aventurine (Opening), Coral Calcite (Amplifier), Leopardskin Jasper (Protection), Moonstone (Balancing), Snowflake Obsidian (Calming), Tiger's Eye (Protection and Grounding)

Flowers: Bee Balm, Birds of Paradise, Morning Glory, Red Hibiscus, Wild Iris

Yoga Poses: Cobra, Triangle, Leg Lifts

Sound: Bam

Mantra: Ong Namo Guru Dev Namo

Affirmations for the Second "Sacral" Chakra

I deserve pleasure.

I belong.

I am exactly where I need to be in my life.

I am perfect just the way I am.

I love and enjoy my body.

I easily allow pleasure and sensuality into my life.

I create easily and effortlessly.

I am passionate.

I feel abundance and pleasure in every moment.

Mental, Emotional, and Physical Aspects of the Second "Sacral" Chakra

Mental/Emotional: This chakra correlates with feelings of creativity or of feeling blocked creatively. This chakra is also related to expressing oneself sexually in a comfortable manner or the feeling of being uncomfortable as a sexual being. This chakra also affects the comfort or discomfort in one's physical body. It relates to the inability or ability to set healthy boundaries in relationships, including expressing our emotions to others and ourselves. This chakra can also house stereotypes regarding what it means to be male and/or female.

If this chakra is not balanced, it can also lead to control issues: the feeling of having to control everything or feelings of not being in control. This chakra is also related to abundance and our ability to create a flow of money in our lives. It is where the seed of creativity is born and relates to how we create. Consequently, it deals with how we create money, relationships, and the control we feel within ourselves.

Physical (Body): The second chakra governs the sexual organs, upper intestines, liver, gallbladder, kidney, stomach, pancreas, adrenal glands, spleen, and middle spine.

If the second chakra is not functioning correctly, it may lead to: lack of satisfying sexual relationships; a very poor self-image; inability to create (physically as well as "creative blocks"); infertility; addictive behaviors; "-itis" diseases; circulatory issues; issues with kidneys, liver, pancreas, spleen, back, and hips.

~~~~~~

Exercise 10: Learning to Step into Creation with the Second "Sacral" Chakra

Before you begin this exercise, I would like you to think of three limiting beliefs you hold relating to your body, money, your sexual relationships, and/or your creativity. These might be statements such as, "I never have enough money," "I always struggle with my weight or determination to exercise," or "I will never find a compatible partner." I also want you to think of the opposite of these limiting beliefs and write both down before you begin. Remember there is a chart at the end of this exercise to help you with it. Please read the whole exercise first before beginning.

As you begin, picture a sun setting. Visualize it as vividly as you can and begin to say the negative beliefs. As you watch the sun set, you release these negative beliefs that you have held in the second chakra about your body, relationships, abundance, and/or creativity. Take a few deep breaths, in and out, understanding that these limited beliefs have stopped you before. However, you can now allow them to be released as you watch the sunset, carrying them with it. Feel what a relief it is to let these beliefs go and take a couple more deep breaths before continuing to allow the relief to wash over your body.

Now, take a breath in and out. This time, visualize a sunrise. See the sun rising, its orange glow beaming, and feel that beginning sunlight on your face, feel it in your lower abdomen. As you picture the sun rising, say the positive affirmations—the statements you came up with that are the opposite of the limiting beliefs you once housed in your second chakra. Know that as the sun rises each day, you too can recreate yourself and these beliefs. Say each belief either aloud or mentally three times each, and breathe in and out slowly each time you say one. Allow these beliefs to wash over you, feel how good they are. See yourself embodying these beliefs and all the goodness that they will bring into your life. Allow the orange glow of the sun rising to penetrate your body; feel it work its way from the tip of your head all the way down to your second chakra. Feel its warm glow abide there. Say thank you for this new day and the power the sunrise possesses, which allows these new beliefs to be deeply planted into your second chakra. Write down what you want to remember about your experience with this exercise.

Exercise 10 Guiding Chart

Limiting Beliefs	Affirmation/ New Belief	Process
1.	1.	1. See the sunset as you breathe and release each limiting belief. Breathe after each and take a few breaths after the sun is down and all are released.
2.	2.	2. Picture the sunrise and say each affirmation three times. Breathing.
3.	3.	3. Feel the glow of the sun from your head traveling down to your sacral chakra. Feel the warm glow and pay gratitude for the new beliefs you have planted.
Relating to your body, money, sexual relationships, and/or your creativity.		

THIRD CHAKRA
The Solar Plexus Chakra

"If you don't stand for something you will fall for anything."

—GORDON A. EADIE

Getting to Know the Third "Solar Plexus" Chakra

You might have heard the expression "there's a fire in your belly." This is a perfect representation of the third, or solar plexus, chakra, which is that fire that guides you and urges you to move forward with power. It is that feeling of being ignited, moving forward with gusto and fighting for what you believe in. It is having utmost confidence in yourself and your causes/beliefs. It is a feeling of self-confidence and knowing you are right. This is how you feel when your third chakra is aligned.

Unfortunately, many people struggle with stepping into their own power, trusting they are on the right path, and claiming with their full strength and knowing, "yes, this is it!" Many people struggle with low self-esteem, fears, and excessive worry, which are all symptoms of the third chakra being underactive. Maybe you have heard limiting statements about yourself and life in general and it seems challenging to claim your full power or even admit that you are powerful. I know I had many similar beliefs and see the same in many of my clients. It is truly a struggle with the ego to admit that you are limitless, claim it, and then begin to take action to prove you are in fact powerful beyond all you have ever imagined. If severely underactive, this chakra can cause a "victim mentality" and a belief that life is happening to us rather than us actively contributing to its twists and turns.

If the third chakra is overactive, power may run your life. This can translate into bullying behaviors, feeling self-centered, and being narcissistic. It can also cause the feeling that you know what is best for everyone else and can make you very controlling over others. This is an overcompensation for the feeling that you are not enough so you have to exaggerate these tendencies to prove that you are. This is not to be judged, just noticed because in noticing your past behaviors you can leave them there, in the past, and choose a new way to move forward.

Some of the physical issues you may develop with an unbalanced third chakra are stomach and digestive problems. If you think about it, this makes sense; your power center, which is your stomach, is not in alignment and it causes physical symptoms in that area. It can create imbalances to the liver, pancreas, and spleen. An imbalanced third chakra can also lead to addiction to work, caffeine, sugar, and beer. You may feel you can prove your power by working harder or non-stop. If you feel so out of touch with your own power it might seem natural to overuse substances so you can numb out or get a boost from another substance instead of looking within for your own power.

Saying affirmations that speak of your unlimited power are a good way to begin to believe and step into the power the third chakra offers. You will learn more about affirmations in "Affirmations" in Section III, but for now I will say the most important part is that when you say them they ring true and do not meet a lot of resistance. You can use the affirmations I mention or adapt ones that feel right and resonate with you. "I AM" affirmations are particularly powerful when balancing this chakra.

The element to this chakra is fire, which you can use to think about how you are feeding your fire to support this chakra. It requires awareness as to what you perceive and feed yourself mentally about success, entitlement, and life situations.

Lions and tigers represent this chakra because they represent courage and power. With a balanced third chakra, you feel that inner power, know you can succeed, and have no doubt that you are unlimited. Courage and standing in your truth and worth also feed this fire as does processing emotions and feeling "I can" and "I AM" instead of letting feelings of low self-esteem dampen the fire and put it out. If this fire is put out, you might feel rejected or stuck so you want to be mindful to feed it with self-encouragement and ways that you are powerful and unlimited. Listening to your gut instincts also fills this fire instead of letting worry overcome you.

Physically eating yellow foods such as sweet peppers, yellow lentils, and corn can feed this third chakra and keep it healthy. Eating sunflower and flax seeds or ginger also helps to keep the fire in the third chakra lit. The yoga pose Fire Breath is very good for keeping this chakra in balance.

This is an important chakra to try to maintain balance in as it controls how you feel about your inner power and ability to move forward in life. Because of this, it is also important to stay in your truth and not lie or misrepresent yourself. Lying will only lead to you having a lower self-respect and separate you from others allowing more judgment and biases. When you stand in your inner power, there is only the need to be your true self because you know this is enough. The more you affirm your powers and unlimitedness, the more the world around you will rise up to meet those expectations.

Notes on the Third "Solar Plexus" Chakra

Sanskrit Name: Manipura

Location: Base of sternum / solar plexus

Element: Fire

Color: Yellow

Glands: Pancreas

Foods: Carbohydrates (pastas, breads, rice, cereal), dairy (milk, cheeses, yogurt), turmeric, cumin, ginger, mint

Crystals: Yellow Topaz (Healing), Yellow Zircon (Balance and Healing), Amber (Protection and Healing), Citrine (Cleansing), Sunstone (Activating), Tiger's Eye (Grounding and Protection)

Flowers: Chamomile, Peppermint, Golden Yarrow, Sunflower

Yoga Poses: The Bow, Fire Breath

Sound: Ram

Mantra: Ananda Hum

Affirmations for the Third "Solar Plexus" Chakra

I am worthy of the very best life.

I am fully in my power.

I am self-disciplined.

I am and all my actions are in integrity.

I trust my gut.

I make good decisions.

I am able to concentrate.

I am unlimited.

I fully process my emotions.

Mental, Emotional, and Physical Aspects of the Third "Solar Plexus" Chakra

Mental/Emotional: This chakra helps us align with our own personal strength and power, our integrity, and self-discipline. Someone who, like a warrior, stands strong and moves forward, is in touch with their feelings, only confronts others when necessary, is rooted in their integrity, and possesses a healthy sense of power.

Physical (Body): This chakra governs the digestive system, pancreas, liver, upper intestines, adrenals as well as the mid-thoracic spine.

If the third chakra is not functioning correctly, it may lead to: a sense of power that is out of balance. It could lead to a bully mentality or on the other end of the spectrum someone who feels like a victim and has no sense of power. It could lead to difficulty concentrating and an inability to make healthy decisions. Physically, the ailments associated with it are any type of digestive issue; problems with the adrenals; anorexia; addictions to caffeine, sugar, or beer; diseases of the liver, pancreas and/or spleen.

~~~~~~

Exercise 11: Finding Your Power Center by Exploring the Third "Solar Plexus" Chakra

I want you to look at the above affirmations and think about what you have learned so far about the third chakra. Next, come up with three affirmations for the third chakra that are as you want to feel. They are especially powerful if they are areas of your life you have wanted to work on. The third chakra is our fire for life and for pursuing our gifts; finding inspiring affirmations will be a powerful first step.

Once you have these three affirmations, I also want you to write down their opposites and have those ready as well. An example is: "I am powerful" and "I don't feel powerful." Remember there is a chart at the end of this exercise to help you with it. Please read the whole exercise first before beginning.

Begin in a quiet space, taking a few breaths to get rooted into the moment. When you are ready, I want you to visualize a fire pit and you lighting the fire with paper on which your powerful affirmations are written. Imagine your affirmations fueling the fire as you strike a match and see them ignite the flames.

Next, see the fire building and know that these powerful affirmations are what helped to build such a healthy and roaring fire. When it is fully lit, see the three negative thoughts written on tiny pieces of paper. Imagine yourself throwing each piece into the fire, knowing that by doing so, you remove that last bit of doubt. Your positive thoughts helped build and fuel the fire. The fire you created helps to destroy those limiting thoughts. Take time to thank yourself for being strong enough to build this fire and say goodbye to these limiting thoughts.

Exercise 11 Guiding Chart

Positive Affirmations	Negative Affirmations	Fire Process
1.	1.	1. See yourself building the fire with big sheets of paper and your positive affirmations written boldly on them.
2.	2.	2. Watch the fire fuel and get bigger with your thoughts and emotions, and the power of how these will be what you emulate.
3.	3.	3. When the fire is roaring, throw the tiny sheets of paper in with your negative thoughts written on them. Know that by doing this you say goodbye to that negative perception and way of being. Thank yourself for taking the time.

FOURTH CHAKRA
The Heart Chakra

"The most painful thing is losing yourself in the process of loving someone too much, and forgetting that you are special too."

—ERNEST HEMINGWAY

Getting to Know the Fourth "Heart" Chakra

The fourth chakra sits in the middle of the seven major chakras. As such, it really brings together the physical side of our existence that our lower three chakras represent as well as the upper three chakras that are about the spiritual side of our existence. It houses our self-worth, self-love, and ability to give and receive love in a healthy manner, with boundaries, and create healthy relationships. This chakra also represents healing of oneself and the love you give to others. As it is in the middle, it is sometimes called the "center" or the "powerhouse" chakra because it brings together both aspects of our existence.

The easiest way to think about and remember aspects of this chakra is to think about love: the love you feel when all is right with the world and you have had a day where everything seemed to flow. Or the love you feel when in the presence of someone you hold dear. You can remember some quotes on love that we have all heard, "love is the answer" and "love is all you need." The key aspect of this chakra is feeling that love and receiving Divine love for yourself. The importance of self-love and how it truly is the base of our happiness is further explored in "Self-Love," in Section III but please keep this in mind as you move forward. It begins with us loving ourselves and only from there can we begin to create relationships with others that we will truly be happy in.

When your heart chakra is underactive you may feel like you have no self-compassion or self-love. Your self-love mirrors to others how you feel you should be treated. If you feel you don't deserve to be loved, you will attract relationships that reflect just that and it will leave you feeling exhausted and depleted. If your heart chakra is underactive, you may feel withdrawn, cold, judgmental, or shy and you won't feel willing or able to be in relationships with others. You may fear intimate relationships, be intolerant of others, or feel very lonely and incapable of having any close relationships; you may feel you do not have enough to offer others.

If your heart chakra is overactive, you may set poor boundaries within relationships or feel very jealous within relationships. An overactive heart chakra can also present as being co-dependent, demanding, possessive, or possibly overly sacrificing, and you may not be setting healthy boundaries. Your heart is so open you feel things overly exaggerated around love; this feeling can cause a need to possess the other person because of the fears you have of the relationship not being there anymore.

Physical issues correlating with the fourth chakra include issues with the heart, lungs, asthma, blood pressure, and sleep. An imbalanced heart chakra can also result in circulatory and respiratory challenges and addictions to chocolate, sugar, or wine. I have seen clients who have presented with breast cancer that have had severe heartbreak; they needed to get to the emotional issues around that relationship to begin to heal. Emotional issues include co-dependency, challenges with care-taking, setting healthy boundaries, feeling bitter about how much you care-take others, and issues around forgiveness.

Eating Mediterranean foods, diet, and aerobic exercise such as daily walks are an excellent way to bring the fourth chakra into balance. Breathing exercises and meditation (see "Meditation" in Section III) also help to bring the heart chakra into balance.

On the emotional level, there are many tools to balance your heart chakra (I offer an exercise in "Self-Love" in Section III for this purpose). Affirmations of your own self-worth and self-love will help bring this chakra into balance. Forgiveness of past relationships and of yourself for challenges in past relationships are also key in bringing the heart chakra into balance so you can move forward with newer, healthier boundaries in place. (Remember the power of Ho'oponopono!)

You want to strive to be a person living with a healthy and balanced heart chakra. Living with a balanced heart chakra offers you the ability to live a life of joy, ease, and flow. Your relationships are healthy; you have a good healthy dose of self-love; and you are forgiving, generous, kind, and compassionate. You feel connected with everything instead of separate and feel a deep sense of belonging and that everything is okay. Being in this space allows life to flow with love, ease, and grace.

Notes on the Fourth "Heart" Chakra

Sanskrit Name: Anahata

Location: Chest, Heart

Element: Air

Color: Green (sometimes gold)

Glands: Thymus (some also say the endocrine gland)

Foods: Mediterranean foods; leafy greens such as kale, spinach; other greens such as avocados, peas, cabbage, and celery

Crystals: Green Aventurine (Healing), Green Kyanite (Healing, Opening Third Eye by Connecting through Heart), Green Tourmaline (Activating and Opening), Emerald (Opening), Rose Quartz (Healing and Opening), Lithium Quartz (Activating, Balancing, Healing), Peridot (Awakening)

Flowers: Holly, Poppy

Yoga Poses: Camel Pose, Cobra Pose, Forward Bend Pose

Sound: Yam

Mantra: Aham Prema

Affirmations for the Fourth "Heart" Chakra

Love is everywhere.

I am love.

I am thinking and feeling lovingly.

I am loving to myself and others.

There is an infinite supply of love.

I am worthy of love.

I freely and easily give and receive love.

I live in balance with others.

I am able to Let Go and Let God.

Mental, Emotional, and Physical Aspects of the Fourth "Heart" Chakra

Mental/Emotional: If this chakra is balanced and aligned, you have healthy relationships with healthy boundaries in place. If underactive, you can feel withdrawn, antisocial, narcissistic, judgmental, cold, or fear intimate relationships. If too open, this can lead to you feeling codependent in relationships or jealous. It can also lead to you feeling possessive, self-sacrificing, and you could have a hard time setting healthy boundaries in relationships. When balanced, you feel self-love and recognize your value and can feel healthy in and out of relationships. You have a balanced and healthy self-esteem, can forgive easily, and feel compassion for others.

Physical (Body): The fourth chakra governs the heart, lungs, breasts, thymus gland, blood pressure, and circulatory and respiratory systems.

If the fourth chakra is not functioning correctly, it may lead to: lung issues and asthma, heart disease, sleep issues, circulatory and respiratory problems; addictions to sugar, chocolate, or wine; poor relationships, lack of self-esteem, feeling depleted, loneliness, holding grudges, lack of forgiveness, not able to feel self-love.

Exercise 12: Falling in Love with Yourself and Creating Healthy Relationships with the Fourth "Heart" Chakra

Following is an exercise to feel and bring your fourth chakra into balance. I also wanted to remind you that Ho'oponopono is one of the most powerful exercises I know to bring this chakra into balance. So if you have the time and willingness, saying a few rounds of Ho'oponopono to yourself and for someone else before or after this new exercise will only make this experience with the fourth chakra more powerful.

To prepare for this exercise, I would like you to come up with:

- Someone in your life you feel a lot of love for and have felt love from.
- A very happy moment in your life involving you and someone else. A time when you felt a lot of love, safe and loved.

- Three affirmations for the heart chakra; these can come from the informational section on the fourth chakra or ones that you come up with that you feel are relevant in your life.

Writing these down may be helpful as then you do not feel the pressure of remembering them. You can also use the chart at the end of this chapter to help guide you through this exercise. Please read the whole exercise first before beginning.

To begin, get in to a quiet space, take a few slow breaths, and sit for one minute getting quiet. Close your eyes and visualize your heart. See it pumping, working continuously for you without you consciously thinking about it. Say a little thank you for this wonderful part of you and now imagine it bathed in green light. Feel the safety and healing powers of this green light as you begin to think of the person you feel love for as well as the situation in your life that brings you such joy. Imagine your heart filling with that love and see it beating a healthy beat and almost expanding because you feel so much love inside yourself.

Stay in this space for a minute, feeling the love you have felt from someone else and feeling this joy that the special moment brought you. Breathe it in and know that these are your special moments and emotions and it is very healing for your heart to remember moments such as these.

Imagine a gold light coming into your heart from outside our body. It can come into your heart any way you like; there is no wrong way. Just know this light is one of great healing and connection. You welcome it into your body to heal whatever might need attention at this moment as you say your three affirmations. Say each one slowly either out loud or silently and feel that gold light entering you as you say each one. Feel the truth in each statement as your heart continues to expand even more—filled with the green and gold lights of healing. Take some breaths and silently repeat those affirmations to yourself. Notice how your body relaxes and feels their truth the more you say them. Feel the warmth these lights have offered your body. Give gratitude to yourself for taking this time to reflect on a person and a time that brought you such love. Give gratitude for yourself for coming up with these three affirmations and for taking the time to breathe them in.

Slowly, when you are ready, know that these affirmations are set in your heart and with a smile, open your eyes.

Please write down what you experienced during this exercise.

Exercise 12 Guiding Chart

Memories/Affirmations	Process
1. _____ (someone you love and feel love from)	1. Green light bathing heart and gratitude.
2. _____ (a happy loving time with someone)	2. Heart pumping and expanding.
3. _____ (affirmations for the heart chakra)	3. Gold light entering the heart, repeating affirmations and feeling gratitude, knowing these are being set deep inside your fourth chakra.

FIFTH CHAKRA
The Throat Chakra

"Just like children, emotions heal when they are heard and validated."
—JILL BOLTE TAYLOR

Getting to Know the Fifth "Throat" Chakra

The power of balancing the fifth "throat" chakra means standing in your truth, being able to communicate effectively with others both in speaking your own mind and truly hearing their point of view. When the throat chakra is aligned, it also offers you unwavering will to stand up for your own truths and determination to walk your path. You stand firmly in integrity when this chakra is in balance and feel all the benefits that offers: in confidence and in being in alignment with your own truth. You can communicate honestly and that offers a freeing feeling.

There are two aspects to this chakra in regards to truth. The yin aspect of the throat chakra is about receiving guidance while the yang aspect is about expressing and voicing truths. The soul speaks to you through this chakra and offers guidance when you are aligned and quiet enough to ask and receive. When this chakra is aligned you are sincere when you speak, assume self-responsibility, and are honest.

If this chakra is underactive, you may be unable to express yourself. You may fear speaking, be shy, or have a challenging time listening to others. You can even be so detached with what your truths are that you feel confused and are unaware of receiving any guidance. When this chakra is overactive, you might speak too much or interrupt often. If this chakra has excessive energy, you might also stutter, speak in defense, or gossip about others. With an overactive fifth chakra, it is possible you can come off as mean to others since you might be speaking out of turn often and excessively.

Physically if your throat chakra is out of balance, you can manifest such illnesses as problems with the thyroid, mouth, and neck. Shoulder and gland issues as well as ear infections and oral addictions are also related to this chakra. You might also feel the need to munch on unhealthy salty snacks when bored or anxious.

Emotionally when this chakra is not aligned, it is very hard to say yes or no as you are unaware of being connected to your guidance. It can also cause a victim mentality, as you may not be seeing the truth of situations and can take them as happening to you instead of realizing you are an active participant. It can cause you to feel out of the flow because you never feel that connection to your guidance system.

You can bring this chakra into balance in many different ways. Affirmations such as "I hear and speak truth" and "I express myself with clear intent" can help you connect with this chakra. Writing letters, singing, and chanting are also ways of bringing this chakra into alignment. Physically drinking water, fruit juices, and herbal teas helps as well as eating tart and tangy fruits such as lemons, limes, grapefruit, and kiwi. The yoga poses of Camel and Bridge are also helpful when connecting with and balancing the fifth throat chakra.

When this chakra is in balance, you will be truly aligned with your creativity and ability to express yourself in many ways. You might begin to hear your guides and inner self speaking to you clearly, guiding you, which is called being clair-audient (more about this in the next chapter). Balanced, it allows for you to be truthful, charismatic, empathic, intuitive, and aware. You are able to keep healthy boundaries by speaking your needs and you voice your opinions with honesty and care. You begin to walk your path in confidence knowing the next step will be revealed when you are ready and you are seen as wise and responsible to the outside world.

Notes on the Fifth "Throat" Chakra

Sanskrit Name: Vishuddha

Location: Throat

Element: Ether

Color: Blue

Glands: Thyroid

Foods: Liquids such as water, herbal teas, natural fruit juices; lemons and limes; other fruits such as apples, apricots, peaches, pears and plums; lemon or lime juice in water.

Crystals: Blue Tiger's Eye (Soothing, Protection), Blue Calcite (Healing), Blue Lace Agate (Balancing), Aqua Aura (Activating and Balancing), Aquamarine (Activating and Clearing), Angelite (Clearing and Healing), Lapis Lazuli (Activating, Balancing and Opening), Turquoise (Balancing and Stimulating)

Flowers: Cosmos, Trumpet Vine, Larch

Yoga Poses: Camel Pose, Bridge Pose

Sound: Gam

Mantra: Purnamidam

Affirmations for the Fifth "Throat" Chakra

I feel safe to communicate my feelings.

I am open, clear, and honest in my communication.

I have a right to speak my truth.

I express myself creatively through speaking, writing, or art.

I know when it is time to listen.

I have integrity.

I express my gratitude toward life.

I listen to my body and my emotions to know what my truth is.

I live an authentic life.

Mental, Emotional, and Physical Aspects of the
Fifth "Throat" Chakra

Mental/Emotional: If the fifth chakra is underactive, you might have a hard time expressing your truth or speaking your mind. You might also have trouble hearing someone else's truth. When the fifth chakra is overactive, you might speak too much, talk out of turn, and gossip. If this chakra is out of balance, it can be challenging to create and express yourself. When the fifth chakra is out of alignment, it also becomes common to judge and criticize yourself and others.

Physical (Body): The throat chakra governs the throat, lungs, trachea, esophagus, neck vertebrae, mouth, teeth, gums, hypothalamus, vocal cords and the thyroid gland.

If the fifth chakra is not functioning correctly, it may lead to: a raspy throat, thyroid issues, chronic sore throats, mouth ulcers, gum difficulties, joint problems, scoliosis, laryngitis, or swollen glands.

~~~~~~

Exercise 13: Connecting to Your Truth and Freedom of Expression with the Fifth "Throat" Chakra

This chakra is one I often find blocked when I work with clients (particularly female clients). It is challenging to speak one's truth all the time and to do so in a kind-hearted way. Many people have learned to silence themselves in certain situations or are the opposite, speaking too much and not really hearing what the other person says. Balancing this chakra brings great power as you can stand in your truth as you speak it and hear what other people really say. It also allows you to create from the full expression of your being.

Before you begin this exercise, I would like you to look at the affirmations in this chapter and pick three positive statements that you would like to be true for you. You could also choose to create similar affirmations you feel reflect what you need to work on to bring this chakra into balance. Know that by saying these and doing this exercise, you bring this into reality and balance this chakra so it can be so.

Once you have those three affirmations written down (writing is an important part of this chakra and in expressing ourselves), please give yourself some time and a quiet space for the following exercise. Sit down with your right hand on your heart and your left hand lightly on your throat. Take a few deep, slow breaths and feel the breath as it travels in and out of your body. Observe how your body feels as this breath comes in and out. Stay with this a minute and observe but do not judge. Imagine a green light at your heart chakra and a blue light at your throat chakra. See them and give yourself time again to imagine the breath coming in and out as you visualize these lights.

Now, say the first affirmation and see it as coming from your heart and coming up to your throat. See that affirmation as surrounded by a bright blue light and affirm that this is your truth. This affirmation has come from your heart, so it must be so. Follow this with the next two affirmations. Say them as many times as you like, each time seeing them come from your heart and up to your throat where they are enveloped by this blue light of truth.

When you are satisfied that these are indeed your new truths, take a few more deep breaths and give yourself gratitude for affirming these new beliefs. Take a few more deep breaths and open your eyes. Please write down your experience during this exercise. As I mentioned, writing and this chakra are directly related. Use the chart below for ease in completing the exercise.

Exercise 13 Guiding Chart

Affirmations	Process
1.	1. See the heart chakra as a green light and the throat chakra as a blue light.
2.	2. As you say each affirmation, see them starting at your heart and working their way up to the throat while being enveloped by the blue light.
3.	3. Affirm each as truth as the blue light envelops it, and show gratitude for each new truth.
Watch your breath, right hand on heart, left hand on throat.	

SIXTH CHAKRA
The Third Eye Chakra

"The intuitive mind is a sacred gift and the rational mind is a faithful servant. We have created a society that honors the servant and has forgotten the gift."

—ALBERT EINSTEIN

Getting to Know the Sixth "Third Eye" Chakra

The third eye chakra is appropriately named as it regulates your inner and outer vision so you can clearly see. When thinking about the sixth chakra, picture what the word "vision" means to you. This chakra helps you see the vision of who you truly can be, release all limits, and look within to dissolve the limits that might have stopped you from moving forward before. When you look inward, you notice the thoughts and patterns that might have been in place for most or all of your life. Noticing these patterns can help you to release old judgments, fear, and programmed beliefs so you can recognize your true power and unlimitedness of being. In noticing, you can reconcile what you truly believe. By releasing the old patterns and knowing the truth of what you currently believe, you allow connection to your own intuition and feel a deep connection with it.

As you begin to look at the patterns, it is important not to judge yourself; be grateful you notice and choose to be aware. There must be a forgiveness for yourself for things you might not have noticed up until this point, and a deep gratitude for the work you are doing now to come into this new awareness. With this new awareness comes the power of consciousness. When you begin to see clearly, you gain confidence and you begin to release some of the fear that has held you back before this moment.

This chakra also controls your outer vision. It keeps in balance the truth of what you experience or "see" in regards to others as well as yourself. If your sixth chakra is underactive, you may have poor memory and sight. You might seem insensitive to others or lack imagination and visualization and not remember your nighttime dreams. If the sixth chakra is overactive, you may have delusions or challenges knowing what is real. You can have delusions of grandeur and actually be connected to Divine Source but have trouble communicating your feelings to others in this world.

The physical symptoms of the sixth chakra not being aligned can be headaches, eyes and ear disorders, nose and sinus issues. An imbalance can cause neurological issues, spinal difficulty, brain tumors, facial nerve problems, learning disabilities, a stroke, seizures, or nightmares. Emotionally when your third eye chakra is out of balance, it can cause addictions to hallucinogens or marijuana that make it difficult to see with correct vision. An imbalance can also cause trouble accessing your intuition and insight, which makes it hard to imagine and see a vision of your future clearly.

You can bring the sixth chakra into balance with such affirmations as "I trust my intuition" and "I am open to the wisdom within." Eating dark fruits such as blueberries and blackberries can help bring this chakra into balance as well as drinking grape juice and red wine. Headstands or balancing postures in yoga can also help open this chakra's energy. Yoga poses to keep this chakra balanced include Eagle, Half Moon, and the simple yet immensely strong yoga pose Tree. Moldavite is a powerful crystal used to open up this chakra, but there are others listed in the information section as well.

A balanced third eye chakra offers inner connection and power. You can feel the oneness with your soul. You trust deeply that you are directed and can tap into this guidance. With this chakra aligned, you truly are all powerful and hold no limits of who you can be and what you can accomplish. Your inner and outer visions are aligned and you hold an unlimitedness of being felt and seen clearly.

Notes on the Sixth "Third Eye" Chakra

Sanskrit Name: Ajna

Location: Center of the forehead about 1 inch above the eyebrows

Element: Light / Dark (Ether)

Color: Indigo

Glands: Pituitary

Foods: Bluish and purple foods such as blueberries, blackberries, green and red grapes, prunes and raisins; drinking juice and wine (in moderation) is also helpful to bring this chakra into balance.

Crystals: Amethyst (Balancing, Opening), Azurite (Opening), Moldavite (Activating, Clearing and Opening), Herkimer Diamond (Activating), Labradorite (Regulating), Ruby Zoisite (Opening)

Flowers: Wild Oat, Queen Anne's Lace, Madia

Yoga Poses: Eagle, Bird of Paradise, Half Moon, Tree

Sound: AUM

Mantra: Shum

Affirmations for the Sixth "Third Eye" Chakra

I trust and follow my intuition.

My inner vision is clear and strong.

I love and accept myself.

I know that all is well in the world.

My life moves effortlessly.

I am in touch with my inner guidance.

I love and accept myself.

I listen to my deepest wisdom.

I nurture my spirit.

Mental, Emotional, and Physical Aspects of the Sixth "Third Eye" Chakra

Mental/Emotional: If the sixth chakra is unbalanced, you may not be able to see the truth of who you really are. You might have low self-esteem or a hugely inflated ego. When the sixth chakra is not in balance, you might be closed to the ideas of others. You might have a challenging time learning and not be in tune with emotional intelligence. You could feel cut off from your intuition or believe you are connected in a way that is inflated and coming from ego.

Physical (Body): This chakra governs the nervous system, eyes, ears, nose, and pituitary gland.

If the sixth chakra is not functioning correctly, it may lead to: brain tumors or brain hemorrhages or a stroke, neurological disturbances, blindness, deafness, full spinal difficulties, learning disabilities, or seizures.

~~~~~~

Exercise 14: Connecting to Your Intuition through the Sixth "Third Eye" Chakra

Most likely you have heard about the "third eye" before and it definitely comes with different connotations. Some feel if your third eye is open you truly see the Universe differently, and you have an ability to see spirits, visions, and much more. We all have different psychic abilities, and balancing the third eye chakra can put you more in touch with these abilities however you receive and perceive them.

"Clairvoyance" means seeing clearly. It is taken from the French word that means "clear seeing." Clairvoyance is an extrasensory ability to perceive distant objects, persons, or events that are not visible through the normal senses. This is the one most commonly portrayed in movies and television shows yet is the rarest of all psychic abilities.

"Clair-audience," like clairvoyance, is made up of two words: "clair" and "audience," which together mean "clear hearing." Clair-audience is the psychic ability to hear sounds and voices that are not audible to common people.

"Clair-sentience" comes from the French word meaning "clear sensing." It involves the intuitive perception of smell, taste, touch, emotions, and physical sensations that contribute to an overall psychic and intuitive impression.

"Clair-cognizant" means clear recognition. People often confuse this with clair-sentience. This is the ability to know something; no one tells you and it is not something you have read before, you just simply know it. It is an inner feeling, gut feeling, something that is just known. It is an ability to answer questions and back them up with facts without prior knowledge.

I wanted to highlight all these different ways we receive intuition and information so that you can get in touch with which way you usually perceive information. This exercise will bring your attention to what is easiest for you as we work with all the senses. Know that these perceptions are like muscles: the more you tell yourself you are open to hearing your intuition and guidance the more you will receive. I receive information mainly through clair-sentience and clair-cognizance though I have had experiences with the others. Working with the one that you receive information from the easiest will allow that connection to deepen. (I have had clients who have had their third eye and clairvoyant abilities open wide while working with me, which can be a little shocking.) Affirm that you are safe and connecting with it for a deeper connection to your intuitive nature to forward your growth and path.

Before beginning this exercise, read over the following affirmations:

- With my sixth chakra balanced, I am open to receiving intuition by seeing visuals or receiving information in my dreams.
- By balancing my sixth chakra, I am open to receiving information by hearing words that guide me.
- My sixth chakra is balanced and healthy, which allows me to be open to receiving information through my senses; receiving physical sensations that tell me the truth of a situation.
- My balanced sixth chakra allows me to be open to receiving guidance by tapping in to my intuition and deep knowing of facts and truths.

Now please get quiet, settled, and take a few breaths. Try and see or feel the location of your sixth chakra (third eye) about an inch above the space between your eyebrows remember that this eye looks in and out so we can see the truth of ourselves and see clearly what our other two eyes might not allow us to see by looking out. Imagine this eye as a mirror or lens: clear, allowing you to see through both front and back. When you can picture it or feel it, now imagine an indigo light coming in and clearing the lens even more. It is bright, indigo, and even though the lens looked clear before you notice as this indigo light works its way over the lens it is getting even clearer. As you notice this cleansing of your inner lens, your third eye, repeat the above affirmations to yourself three times each.

After this exercise, write down how it felt and which affirmation resonated the most. You might have felt a tingling when you said one of them or a deep sense of knowing that this is how you receive information. Working with this exercise more than once will allow the sixth chakra to be cleansed and balanced and will set the intention of you wanting a clearer connection to your intuition. The following chart will help guide you through the exercise.

Exercise 14 Guiding Chart

Affirmations	Process
1. With my sixth chakra balanced, I am open to receiving intuition by seeing visuals or receiving information in my dreams.	1. Take a few breaths and locate your sixth chakra by visualizing it or feeling it there.
2. By balancing my sixth chakra, I am open to receiving information by hearing words that guide me.	2. See your sixth chakra as a lens or mirror.
3. My sixth chakra is balanced and healthy, which allows me to be open to receiving information through my senses; receiving physical sensations that tell me the truth of a situation.	3. Imagine an indigo light coming in and surrounding the sixth chakra.
4. My balanced sixth chakra allows me to be open to receiving guidance by tapping in to my intuition and deep knowing of facts and truths.	4. See the indigo light clearing the sixth chakra as you say the affirmations three times each. Give thanks for the clearing of the sixth chakra, which allows you to connect further to your intuition.

SEVENTH CHAKRA
The Crown Chakra

"No man is great enough or wise enough for any of us to surrender our destiny to. The only way in which anyone can lead us is to restore to us the belief in our own guidance."

—HENRY MILLER

Getting to Know the Seventh "Crown" Chakra

The seventh chakra connects us to all that is. When learning about this chakra, it helped me to think about trees, animals, and nature. No one has to tell them how to grow or survive, yet they just do. We are all connected to Divine information and can receive this information directly. You can have a direct line for knowledge and guidance and see, hear, feel, and intuit very clearly. The challenge to receiving all of this information and guidance is to truly live in the now. Section III is devoted to ways to connect to the present moment, and the power and knowledge you receive by doing this is limitless. There has to be a willingness to not live in what has happened in the past or what you think might happen in the future but to truly be in this moment and live from there. The energy from all our prayers and intentions, combined with our thoughts and feelings, stores itself in the crown, as prana, which is Divine energy and is powerful, intuitive, and healing.

If the seventh chakra is underactive, you could feel disempowered and like you have no choices available to you. You might make the same decisions repeatedly, place blame on others, and be unable to hear your own voice. When the crown chakra is overactive, you could have delusions of power and try to manipulate and control others. You might try to overpower others with your thoughts and actions that are energetically unaligned with your soul.

The physical symptoms of the seventh chakra being misaligned include migraine headaches, sensitivity to light, exhaustion, and laziness. The emotional symptoms could be thinking of the future with distress and fear. A misalignment in this chakra may also cause you to be unable to commit and understand spirituality. You might have a limited vision of life, and feel exhausted and that life is challenging. You might also fear being abandoned, feel very alone, and have a very limited view on life. You could have trouble seeing the greater picture and not have faith that you will be led forward with guidance.

To align this crown, you need to get into the current moment by using tools such as meditation or prayer. You need to set aside time to connect with your soul and listen. You need to learn how to quiet your mind, let go of the noise around you; then you will begin to hear your inner guidance and feel your connectivity to all else. The more you do this, the deeper and easier you will feel that connection. To align this chakra, it is not so much about what you eat but how you eat. You need to be in the present moment and show gratitude for the food and drink you are ingesting. You can fast or be very cognizant of what you have decided to eat and drink; showing the awareness of how food affects your body helps align your seventh chakra. Flowers, crystals, and herbs that help align this chakra are listed in the informational section. The yoga poses that help with connecting are Savasana, Tree, and Sat Kriya.

When the crown chakra is in alignment, your energy flows with ease and you feel Divinely led. You feel connected to all and to guidance; you live from the moment, can get out of your head, and simply "be" present. When you are in this state of flow, you can move through life with confidence and grace and truly be connected to the inner you and the unlimitedness that it offers.

Notes on the Seventh "Crown" Chakra

Sanskrit Name: Sahasrara

Location: Crown of the head

Element: (Thought/Space) Ether

Color: Violet

Glands: Pineal

Foods: Herbs (frankincense, juniper, myrrh, copal, and sage); practice mindfulness when eating; be aware and pay gratitude for the food that you are fortunate enough to be ingesting.

Crystals: Celestite (Aligning, Balancing, Opening), Amethyst (Clearing and Balancing), Clear Topaz (Activating), Clear

Quartz (Aligning, Balancing, Clearing), Rutilated Quartz (Balancing, Clearing), Selenite (Balancing)

Flowers: Lotus, Angelica, Star Tulip

Yoga Poses: Savasana, Tree, Sat Kriya

Sound: OHM

Mantra: Vedohum

Affirmations for the Seventh "Crown" Chakra

I am Divinely Guided and Protected.

I seek experiences that nourish my spirit.

I am part of the Divine.

I listen to the wisdom of the Universe.

I trust my intuition.

I live in the present moment.

My life moves with grace.

I honor the Divine within me.

I am connected with the wisdom of the Universe.

Mental, Emotional, and Physical Aspects of the Seventh "Crown" Chakra

Mental/Emotional: If the seventh chakra is balanced, you have a trust of life and an ability to see the larger picture and how we are all connected. With the seventh chakra balanced, you have faith and inspiration and a sense of your life's purpose. If your seventh chakra is overactive, you can feel delusional with power and try to control others and situations. If your seventh chakra is underactive, you can feel a lack of power and that you have no choices. You could place blame on others and make the same decisions and relive the same patterns.

Physical (Body): The seventh chakra governs the muscular and skeletal systems, skin, right eye, cerebrum, and pineal gland.

If the seventh chakra is not functioning correctly, it may lead to: issues with the central nervous system, energetic disorders, depression, chronic exhaustion not linked to a disease, and extreme sensitivity to light and/or sound.

Exercise 15: Connecting with the Guidance and Wisdom of the Universe through the Seventh "Crown" Chakra

The seventh chakra is truly the chakra that has us aligned and connected with all. Most of us have been taught we are separate, but nothing could be further from the truth. We all have access to Divine Guidance and with that comes such power because we no longer have to feel alone. If we can quiet our minds enough to let this guidance come through us, we will be guided to make decisions that lead to the life of our dreams.

I want you to pick three affirmations from the previous chapters or some of your own that go along with this chakra. Some of my personal favorites include "I am connected with the wisdom of the Universe," "I am Divinely guided and protected," and "I live in the present moment." You can use these or any three that resonate most deeply with you.

Get quiet, all noise or potential noise put aside, phones turned off and watch your breath. Take some time to really sink into this present moment. I love the idea of putting all your worries in a box next to you and closing the lid. They will be there when you end this exercise, but for now you can leave them aside. Take some more breaths, noticing how you feel lighter with these challenges and worries temporarily put aside.

Close your eyes and imagine a violet light coming in through your crown. This light has all the information and connection you could ever ask for. See if you can feel the tingle in your crown and know this is a confirmation of you receiving pure informational and guiding energy.

As you feel that purple light warming your crown, say the affirmations either out loud or to yourself three times each. Say them and feel them as true as you notice your head tingling and that violet light focused on your crown.

I now want you to say "thank you" to the Universe for this connection, for guiding you and letting you know you are never truly alone. Say it a few times and observe how it makes you feel. When you are ready, open your eyes. Please write at least a few sentences about your experience with this exercise. Use the following chart as a guide.

Exercise 15 Guiding Chart

Affirmations	Process
1.	1. Imagine your challenges being out in a box beside you and shut the lid. Take some deep breaths, centering in to this present moment.
2.	2. Imagine a violet light coming in to the crown of your head. Say the affirmations with that light centered on your crown.
3.	3. Say "thank you" to the Universe for this connection, for guidance, and for the knowledge you are never truly alone.

SECTION II
CONSIDERATIONS

As you can see, the chakras are an important part of your health, well-being, and energy system. There is such power in understanding your chakras, and therefore, understanding how your body communicates with you. The more you tune in and take assessment of your own health, emotional and physical, the more answers you will receive on how to improve it. If you feel unbalanced, ask yourself which chakra is related to this feeling and see if doing the chakra exercise provides help to bring you and it into balance.

You need not remember everything about each chakra; this book is a resource you can continually go back to. You can also read one of Cyndi Dale's many books or encyclopedias on chakras if you find these resonate deeply with you and you want to learn more.

Often, you will find there are one or two chakras that need more attention than the rest. We each have our own strengths and challenges, patterns and behaviors in many different areas of our lives. By being cognizant of your energy body and setting the intention that you want to be able to hear the messages being sent to you, you are much more likely to receive that guidance. Again, be kind with yourself in this process. You are learning a lot and this is a process of healing old wounds that might run deep. Every time you do an exercise or take this time for yourself, you affirm to yourself that yes, you are very ready for change. That taking of action deserves gratitude toward yourself and a hearty pat on the back! Next, I will teach you ways to stay in the present moment, which truly is the way to stay in flow and access your guidance in any moment.

SECTION III
Staying in the Present Moment

"Between stimulus and response there is a space. In that space is our power to choose our response. In our response lies our growth and our freedom."

—VIKTOR FRANKL

The present moment is truly all we ever have, but we are rarely able to remain in the moment. We are usually in our heads, ruminating over something that happened in our past or worrying about something that might happen in the future. In Section I, you learned how to shed things from your past and tune into the present moment. In Section II, you learned just how valuable it is to tune into your energy body for answers as to what is going on emotionally and physically within you. Section III provides tools that offer ways to stay present. In noticing all the gifts of the moment, and that in most moments you are totally safe and everything is just fine, you switch the way your body and mind react to everything around you. You will not react from some past pattern or belief but can rather choose, consciously, how you want to react and what is appropriate. In being present, you create your reality rather than letting your past stories create a repeat of the same experiences. There is such power and strength in this as you will soon see! Your path to "presence" needs to begin with the most important aspect to your well-being, self-love.

SELF-LOVE

"Loving yourself ... does not mean being self-absorbed, it means welcoming yourself as the most honored guest in your own heart."

—MARGO ANAND

The most important person in your life is yourself. Yet, if you are like most, you probably put yourself last or near the bottom of the "to care for" list. You need to know that you are worthy of love. That love begins with you. You are a mirror reflecting to others how they should treat you. When you are filled with self-doubt, angst, and worry, you are not your best self and you might feel as if you are in eternal stuck mode. When you are grateful and allow yourself to feel love for yourself, the people and situations around you begin to reflect just that.

Most of us were taught and told not to be egotistical. But self-love is not at all egotistical; it is simply about knowing our value. When we know our self-worth, our lives can be in flow, and we can operate out of a place of security rather than self-doubt and worry.

As humans, we can be pretty rotten to ourselves. We can fill our brains and hearts with negative self-talk, sometimes not even hearing the constant barrage of comments slung our way from our inner programming. Some or most of the words might not even be truly believed, as discussed in "Negative Self-Talk" in Section I, and in reading about the first chakra. They can be words you have heard about yourself in the past that have made it into your "background recording." The good news is that you can change those recordings. The first step is to hear them and take notice. The second is to replace them with more loving and kind thoughts for yourself.

The negative thoughts you say to yourself can seem so powerful, but the good news is that they can be replaced—it may simply take a little time and patience. I promise it won't take as long to replace them as the numerous years the negative thoughts have been in place. When you begin to choose your thoughts, instead of just having them on automatic pilot, they are so much more powerful than those "programmed" thoughts. You can see your life change pretty quickly by eliminating one negative self-belief at a time. For example, you might have grown up thinking, hearing, or feeling you weren't "smart enough" to do something. Now, you truly understand that you have the capacity to excel at many different challenges and tasks. If that thought in itself brings up resistance, take a second to think of all you have already accomplished in your life that required thought and action-taking. In removing that negative belief and replacing it with kind, loving thoughts and encouraging words to yourself, you will not only say you are smart enough but will feel that shift inside you and the resonance of truth in it rather than the disappointment and feeling of lack of power the first belief created.

You can also look at it this way: if someone yelled at you and berated you, would that motivate you or would a kind nudge and unconditional love work better for you? As humans, there is a tendency to berate ourselves, which only puts us in a state of low self-esteem and can make us feel unmotivated to do anything. When you relate to yourself with the same loving kindness you offer to your loved ones, you will begin to find inner strength you might not have known was even there!

At soul level, you are perfect. Every single experience you have is one you can learn from. Sometimes the ones labeled negative are in fact the very ones that teach the most. We can lie awake saying to ourselves we wish we said or did something differently or even that we wish someone else did something differently; but each and every moment can be learned from. When you stop judging yourself and introduce into your life the following tools (such as "Gratitude," also in this section), you can feel this internal shift. There is a reason Ho'oponopono is so powerful. Through it, you affirm your love for yourself, forgiving yourself for your humanness and any way you have contributed to your current state of mind and being, and give yourself permission to be okay. You always have that option of knowing you are okay and celebrating instead of insulting yourself.

You need to treat yourself as you would your closest loved ones! Give the same amount of respect and love to yourself as you would someone else. We all deserve unconditional love, and at soul level we know this. When you nurture and love yourself, the world changes in response. The people you meet are kinder, more "synchronicities" begin to happen, your path seems to open before you, and you certainly smile a heck of a lot more.

Exercise 16: Opening Up to Self-Love

I would like to guide you in a simple exercise in self-love. To prepare, you'll need to think of:

- a person you feel tremendous love for; a friend, spouse, child, family member, or anyone else that when you think of them your heart grows warm; and

- something you give yourself a hard time or beat yourself up about. Maybe it has been a struggle with weight loss. Maybe it's difficulty finding financial stability. Maybe you tend to procrastinate. It could be you feel badly about a relationship issue. You know what you give yourself a hard time about; choose one challenge.

Once you have these two things in place, try these five steps:

1. Take a few seconds to notice your breathing...don't change it—simply notice it. This helps you become totally present and in the moment. You can count

your in and out breaths if this helps you get to a more centered state of presence.

2. Imagine the loved one whom you picked. Feel what it is like when they are around you or you are speaking with them. Engage your senses and truly feel that person is with you. Feel the love you feel for each other. See them in your mind's eye. If they bring a certain scent to memory, engage that as well. The more you can feel them with you the better.

3. Now, imagine that your loved one is approaching you about the issue that you chose, which you find challenging. Your loved one is coming to you for your love and advice about this same issue that they now have as their own.

4. Picture yourself giving your loved one advice from your heart. When we truly love someone, we are able to be non-judgmental. We know their challenge is not as bad as it seems, as we are able to comfort them and show them love and support.

5. Now, apply this advice to your situation—it will help you rise above the challenge a bit and put your challenging issue into a more manageable perspective.

6. Feel the love that the loved one gives you for your advice and for you being there for them. You always have the ability to give that same love and gratitude to yourself. Give yourself gratitude for taking this time

to connect with the unconditional love that you have for yourself.

This exercise may take as little as a few seconds, or as much as a few minutes. See if you can notice the next time you say hurtful or demeaning things to yourself. Do not beat yourself up about saying them, as that is the first step to change, and it's a step to be celebrated. Write about your experiences during this exercise.

Recognizing that you had a mean thought about yourself should not be another thing to be mad at yourself for. The more you stop and notice, the sooner it will become second nature to change your words to yourself, and the sooner you will start to treat yourself with a little more love and kindness!

This journey of self-love will be continual; be kind to yourself in this process. Falling in love with yourself is truly the most important and beautiful thing you can do to see your life transform.

AFFIRMATIONS

"You've been criticizing yourself for years, and it hasn't worked. Try approving of yourself and see what happens."

—LOUISE HAY

Affirmations are sentences you say to yourself to affirm how you want to be, feel, or what you want to attract into your life. They are phrases you repeat over and over, if need be, to assure your soul and inner self that you desire and know you are more than you have given yourself credit for up until this point. Using affirmations is an effective way to switch moods and dissolve patterns and unwanted behaviors. All affirmations are not created equal, in my opinion. Coming up with affirmations that resonate with your soul and repeating them is a powerful way to transform many aspects of your life, from your health and financial situation, to relationships and emotions, to how you see yourself on a daily basis.

You know from earlier chapters that you always send yourself messages. Each moment, your thoughts and emotions talk and relay information. Most of these thoughts are unconscious, and you usually react accordingly from a place in which you are not even aware of them or hearing them. The words you tell yourself, along with the emotions they bring up, are like a constant prayer to the Universe. Whether you are praying for what you want or don't want is usually the question. When you are in the present moment and notice what your usual inner-dialogue is, you can choose to change it to something more positive.

The unconscious rattling of thoughts that your mind tends to engage in will help shape the world around you, if that is all you are offering. When you begin to notice and take charge of some of the thoughts that you send yourself consciously, the world can change to reflect those thoughts and emotions. Your conscious words to yourself are so much more powerful than the unconscious babbling rooted in the past. I look at it as fine-tuning a radio station. Usually we send the Universe static with our emotions and thoughts going all over the place. Setting affirmations and being in the present moment to say them is a good way of fine-tuning that channel and sending a clear message. Affirmations are a wonderful way of looking at what you want, who you want to be, and what you want to bring in to your life, and it begins to put those words out to the Universe.

I offer one caution before you begin saying affirmations. This is a topic debated by some, but I feel it is very important. At some level, I feel you must believe your affirmation is possible. I have seen people say affirmations that bring up resistance and, in some cases, they begin to actually attract the opposite of what they are affirming. Your subconscious mind also hears your words and if it does not agree, you might be bringing up some old wounds and feelings of unworthiness. Consequently, the Universe might begin to show you the things you are most afraid of.

When I was healing myself, I could not have simply said to myself, "I am healed" or "I feel no pain," because these phrases were simply not true at that time. My body and subconscious mind would have seen that discrepancy, and I feel they would have caused huge resistance within me. Instead, I said believable affirmations such as, "I am working on feeling better every day," "I am grateful for all I am learning about the mind-body connection," "I am happy I have so many resources to teach me how to feel better." These all resonated deep within me as truth. The more I said them and felt the gratitude and joy from repeating them, the more I felt myself feel lighter and healthier. Within three weeks, I was healed of all disease. I fully believe that the affirmations, and specifically them being believable, helped me tremendously to heal.

"I AM" statements are particularly powerful. You affirm to your soul what you are. You have beliefs you know are true at soul level, mentally and emotionally. However, you also probably have been told the opposite. Beliefs that resonate as truth do not bring up resistance, and I have found these to be the most powerful. One of my favorite sets of affirmations is, "I am unlimited," "I know no limits," "There are no limits to what I can create." It is possible, when I began this course of study, that these might have brought up some resistance. But now they are words I know are true and resonate deeply. Not only have I seen in my own life unlimitedness of being but also in the lives of many of my clients and the people I surround myself with. When you begin to formulate affirmations, hold your hand on your heart as you say them out loud and see if they bring up resistance or a deep sense of truth.

I want to repeat again the importance of keeping affirmations real. If it is money you want, saying, "I am a millionaire" when you are struggling to pay your bills and are out of work will probably bring up resistance. Instead, you can say things such as, "I am learning ways to earn more money each day," or "I am attracting money and situations for me to receive more money." What you keep repeating in your conscious mind is like praying for what you want. When you stop sending out negative or mixed signals, choose what you want to create, and claim who you are, it gives you a clear channel for manifestation the Universe provides.

I also recommend to state affirmations in a positive form. Instead of saying "I don't want to be sick anymore," an affirmation would be "I am working on improving my health every day." You don't want to concentrate on words that bring up any angst such as "sick," "poor," or "depressed"; keep the statements as positive as possible and have them free of negative words.

There is no right or wrong way or number of times you should say affirmations. Any time is better than no time. I feel they are even more powerful when you say them in the mirror. They are powerful when you say them before you go to bed or when you get up in the morning. Affirmations are also more powerful when you put emotion into them. If you say, "I am going to have a great day" but are simultaneously going through all the things in your mind that you are dreading, you are not supporting the affirmations with emotion. Take a few minutes each day—in the shower, or when you are getting ready, for example—and say your affirmations. When you tell yourself positive affirmations on a regular basis, you feel your vibration get higher, your limitations disappear, and you will create the synchronicities aligned with what you affirm you want to create. You truly can create your reality, and affirmations are a wonderful way of validating this for yourself.

Exercise 17: Expanding Your Sense of Self and Reality with Affirmations

I would like you to think of two areas of your life where you want to see change and growth. These can be relationally, financially, spiritually, mentally, emotionally, or physically. Once you have those two areas, think of three specific affirmations for each that resonate deeply within you. Remember that the chapters in Section II also have affirmations you can choose from. Put your hand on your heart as you try them out. You can also try saying them in front of a mirror. Do these affirmations bring up confidence and a smile or resistance and discomfort? I would also like for you to have at least one "I AM" statement for each area. Possible examples for each include:

Relationally: I am ready to share my love with someone. I am setting healthy boundaries in all my relationships. I am attracting like-minded people to me.

Financially: I am open to creating new streams of income in my life. I am working toward my financial goals every day.

Spiritually: I connect with my Higher Self every day. I am always open to receiving Divine Guidance.

Mentally: I learn something new every day. I read often and understand everything I read.

Emotionally: I am in touch with and honor my emotions. I speak my truth in my relationships.

Physically: I am conscious of everything I put in my body and consistently make healthy choices. I exercise and feel wonderful.

An alternative way to do these is to write out a few affirmations and see how it feels. Play with them. Does it feel most powerful for you when writing them, speaking them out loud in front of a mirror, or speaking them to yourself? Do they bring up resistance, or are you feeling more confident as you say them? Take notice and write down the experiences you have and your preferred method of processing affirmations. Recognize that the affirmations and the process you use to communicate them may change, but for now, do what is most comfortable for you.

GRATITUDE

"Gratitude bestows reverence, allowing us to encounter everyday epiphanies, those transcendent moments of awe that change forever how we experience life and the world."

—JOHN MILTON

Gratitude is one of the most powerful tools for being in the present and for bringing more goodness into our lives. We all love and appreciate hearing those words "thank you" after we do something nice for someone. We have almost come to expect those words when we do something for someone or pay a compliment, and yet we seldom say them unless something is specifically handed to us or done for us. Yet, we receive gifts from the Universe all the time. We wake up each day able to breathe, and most of us are able to walk, taste, feel, see, hear, eat, drink, and appreciate so much of what the world has to offer. We have people who love us and who we love deeply and have become used to them "being there." Most of us have a safe place to live. We can take these huge gifts for granted, instead of truly appreciating them. In paying gratitude and saying thank you for all the Universe has to offer and for our own special gifts, we can truly see the Universe offers us even more to be grateful for!

Gratitude was one of the most important tools I utilized to heal myself from several chronic illnesses and disease. Since then, I have incorporated it as an important part of my daily routine. In the morning, before my feet hit the floor, and in the evening, before I shut my eyes, I take some time to reflect on something, someone, or several things I am grateful for. I don't make it the same each time. Instead I take those few seconds or minutes to bask in the beauty and blessedness of what I am paying gratitude for in that moment. I give it my full attention and feel it deeply with my heart. It is easy for us to get so caught up in what isn't right and to worry about the past or the future. In paying gratitude, you bring yourself fully into the present moment; and by paying attention and giving that praise of what is good, you invite the Universe to bring more of it into your life. Start paying gratitude every day, and you can truly watch your life transform in ways you could not have imagined. This is also a wonderful habit to instill in the children in your life. I say prayers with my daughter nightly, and we incorporate what we were grateful for that day and it always brings up smiles and positive feelings.

Gratitude is one of the most powerful tools I know for shifting energy around any situation or relationship. So many times we focus on what we don't want, don't like, or worry about what the future will bring. We judge situations and deem them "bad" and also are our own toughest critics. We become wrapped up in our own minds and patterns of thought and sometimes days, weeks, or even longer periods of time pass without us taking that time to truly feel gratitude for all the things working well in our lives.

Gratitude is so powerful because you not only express love but also offer a heartfelt thank you to the Universe. You show your appreciation and that truly makes room for even more goodness to come into your life. What you focus on expands, and when you take time to think about what and who you appreciate, it truly adds a powerful energy and elevates your mood instantaneously.

It is also important to give gratitude for ourselves. We certainly beat ourselves up enough; we should take time to give ourselves the recognition and appreciation we deserve. Showing gratitude to yourself is a helpful way to begin to feel self-love. In the process of transformation and change, this is an important step. You may show gratitude for anything you want in your life, and by all means make it fun! Give yourself gratitude for doing the exercises in this book, for not losing your temper in a situation you normally would have, for not taking that fifth cookie, for smiling at someone in the supermarket and making their day, for knowing you are trying to change your life for the better—the list is never-ending. There is always something to be grateful to yourself for!

Having been so ill for more than six years, I remember clearly how easy it is to be caught up in all the things I couldn't "do, be, or have in my life" instead of focusing on what I did have. I still maintain that gratitude was one of the most instrumental tools that allowed me to heal myself in three short weeks. I needed to switch my inner dialogue from the long list of "can'ts," for example, "I probably can't drive my kids today because I am so dizzy," "I am too ill and nauseous to run errands," and "I will have to decline another invitation because I am in so much pain." Instead I would say gratitude for the goodness in my life, for example, "I am so happy my kids are healthy," "I am so grateful it is a beautiful day out and the sun in shining," and "I am grateful I can lie in bed and read." Whatever your situation may be, there is always something to be grateful for!

There are several ways I have found to be effective at bringing the magical energy of gratitude into your life. You could make a list of ten things you are grateful for in your life and ten things you are grateful for in yourself. You could keep a gratitude list, and write down little things as they come up, or make it a daily habit. You can tell someone you care about how grateful you are for him or her or something that person did for you. There are countless ways to express gratitude verbally or with your actions, to yourself or others. The following are two exercises I have found useful. One is to pay gratitude to yourself, and the other is to feel the gratitude you have for someone or something that has been in your life. In the morning or before bed, the mind is in its most receptive state as we are on the verge of consciousness mixed with sleep. It is also the time we are known to worry. Use this time to take a minute or two and think deeply about what you are grateful for and all the aspects that make that person or situation a gift in your life. Gratitude can truly shift energy easily, and if you keep with it, you will begin to see the results and watch more positive energy and healthiness come in to your life.

Exercise 18: Connecting to Gratitude for Yourself and Others

Gratitude for Someone or Something

Take some time and think about one thing or one person you are very grateful for. Feel it—every reason, everything you love about that person or thing. Spend at least a minute or two going through all the reasons and everything you are grateful for about that person or thing. Now, close your eyes and imagine that person or thing in front of you and see yourself paying thanks. If it is a person, see them receiving it and how happy it makes them to hear your words. You might even decide to do this in person or call or write someone, letting them know how grateful you are for them. Write down the feelings you experienced during this exercise.

Gratitude for Yourself

Take a moment and get quiet and pay attention to your breath. Thank yourself for taking this time and for the work you have been putting in to changing your life. Next, imagine your Higher Self there with you, thanking you for all the wonderful things you have been doing. It means so much to your soul when it is acknowledged. Just as we love to pay thanks to people who have done nice things for us, it is just as important to give thanks to ourselves. Thank yourself for all the qualities and characteristics you are grateful for. See your Higher Self smiling and feel their love for you. (Feel their appreciation for acknowledgement and an inner hug along with their unconditional love.) Gratitude is the most powerful emotion I know, because it is pure love and also appreciation combined. That thankfulness is such an affirmation to the Universe that you appreciate what you have, and it is a surefire way of encouraging the Universe to give you even more to be grateful for.

Notice how these exercises made you feel and take a moment to write about them. Gratitude has a way of making people feel warm and happy. Your soul is happy and the Universe responds positively when you take that time to show your appreciation for yourself and all the wonderful things life has to offer you right now, in this present moment.

ENERGY HEALING

"If you want to find the secrets of the universe, think in terms of energy, frequency and vibration."

—NIKOLA TESLA

We are all self-healing, and we are all made of energy, whether that energy is called "chi," "prana," "mana," "ki," or any other name. Eastern and ancient medical models have been based on energy for thousands of years. Western medicine chose to concentrate on the mechanics and biology of the body, which of course are important too. But the major aspect missing from that medical model is that we are made of energy and can use that energy to notice where we are physically (as learned in the chakra chapters) and also to heal. Many cultures base their medicine on energy; an example is acupuncture, which I have seen help myself and countless clients. All these traditions and cultures recognized the importance of naming this very important part of us, our essence, and what regulates our body.

We witness our body's ability to heal itself when small cuts heal. This is coupled with our expectation, "this will heal," because it has been proven to us countless times in our lifetime. We don't have anyone telling us how bad it is or that the chances of healing are slim to none. But when we get a more serious illness, all our limiting beliefs that we have learned come to the surface and affect our body's ability to heal itself.

One of the most important quotes I heard from the movie *The Secret*, is that the body is 99.999 percent new every eleven months. The body always creates new cells. It made sense to me that where my attention, energy, and emotions went would contribute to whether or not my body made "happy and healthy cells" or "sick and diseased cells." It was challenging to do this when I felt like I had the flu most days, and the doctors told me I would not get any better. Yet, one of the first things I did, when I decided I could feel better, was to focus my energy on the parts of my body that did not hurt and pay gratitude for them. By shifting my attention and paying gratitude for what sometimes was just my little finger not being in pain, I told the Universe, "Yes I do have healthy cells and I know if this part of me feels okay then other parts can as well." I would literally feel so much better and be able to get out of bed, when other days I had struggled to do so. But it made so much sense. Where our energy is focused is where it will flow. Waking up and telling myself how sick or how in pain I felt was not helping!

Tuning into your energy body is easy, quick, and can improve your emotions and health in a few moments. When you tune into your energy body with your intention, you truly improve your life, physically, mentally, emotionally, and spiritually. This energy is always available to you. Not only is your own body made up of energy, but so is everything on this planet. When you tap into your own energy body, you can consciously feel the energy of other people and objects around you.

Self-healing with energy is not complicated. In a few simple steps, you can bring a feeling of peace into your body. You can tune into your energy body and use your thoughts and emotions to change the frequency and flow of your energy. In doing this, even for only a few minutes, you can feel your body relax and feel physical changes occurring within. Yes, there are many modalities of healing that you can get trained in, and I encourage that strongly if you find one that resonates with you. But we all have this self-healing energy we can tap into without any training—we just need to remember and focus our attention and intention.

It is as simple as changing the channel from a negative reporting news channel to your favorite comedy show and feeling yourself relax with that fresh perspective. Your day can move in a new direction that will guarantee you invite ease, flow, and even "miracles" into your life. You choose your thoughts consciously and, therefore, change where you want the energy to flow in your life.

Exercise 19: Feeling Energy in Your Body and Using It to Heal Yourself

Here are five easy steps you can do in five to ten minutes. Please read through all steps, and then take the next few minutes to put the wheels in motion and practice! If you feel inspired to stay in this state for longer, by all means do!

1. Sit in a comfortable position and become aware of your breath. There is no need to change it. Pay attention to the flow of your breath—in and out, in and out. No judging it, no changing it—just noticing. This is simply to become "present" and to stop some of the never-ending thoughts from interfering for the next few minutes. Count your breaths in and out if that helps you to center and calm your mind.

2. Take your hands (palms together) in front of you and rub them together quickly for thirty to sixty seconds. Let them become warm from the friction and feel that warmth. Invite a slight smile in as you rub your hands. Smiling itself is healing and has the ability to improve your mood in a few seconds.

3. Hold your hands six to eight inches away from each other, facing each other and feel the energy flowing through them. This energy is always here, you feel it now because of the intention and due to the awakening of your awareness to it. As you feel this energy, tune into it, know this is part of you. Keep on smiling—doesn't this feel pretty cool? If the feeling of the energy wanes, rub your hands together again. There is no one judging how you do this. This is fun and is all about what is comfortable for you. Even if you feel silly (which, believe me, I felt silly at first), that's a good thing as it will have you

smiling and feeling lighter. This energy can feel like warmth, tingles, or a magnetic connection between your hands—whatever you feel is right and appropriate for you.

4. When you feel the energy in your hands, close your eyes. See if you can move the energy up your arms, through your body. There is no wrong way to do this. You awaken your energy body with your intent, and your intent is to feel and to heal.

   See if you can move that energy to whatever part of your body you may have some stress or dis-ease in. Keep it there, knowing you are sending it love and positive healing energy. If you feel like you lost touch with the energy, rub your hands together again. There is no judgment and no way to do this wrong. You can picture the energy in whatever manner feels right for you. Perhaps you just want to feel it; maybe you want to picture it as a white light—it is whatever way feels the easiest for you. Let yourself play with this step and smile while doing it.

5. Continue to work with this flow of energy. Call it to different parts of your body. Notice how it feels as it reaches different spaces. Know that this energy can help those areas that usually bring you pain. Feel the gratitude for finally recognizing this inherent ability in you.

Notice the energy relaxing the parts of the body it flows into. Thank your body for awakening to this awareness and healing. Playing with this energy flow, for even a few minutes, can bring a state of joy and peace that you felt was impossible even mere minutes earlier.

How did that feel? I know when I first felt energy, I was pretty amazed that it was always present in my body, even though I had not been consciously aware of it. Play with this, have fun, and write down what you notice and how you feel before and after this exercise.

MEDITATION

"Meditation can help us embrace our worries, our fear, our anger; and that is very healing. We let our own natural capacity of healing do the work."

—THICH NHAT HANH

When we hear the word "meditation," several images immediately come to mind. You might think of the yogi on a mountain sitting in the lotus position with his fingers in a mudra saying, "Om." You might imagine you need to "clear your mind" and believe that to be an impossible task. Meditation, simply, is being in the present moment and allowing yourself no distractions. In this quiet, we receive guidance and solutions where before we only found struggle. Meditation is good for relieving stress, reducing illness, and living a happier life in general. In my own journey and with the lives of my clients, I have found meditation (and the several different ways we can bring it in to our lives) to be priceless in creating the life we desire.

There are many different types of meditation. This chapter touches on the ones I have found most useful for myself and in working with my clients. There is no one right way to meditate for all people.

Sometimes one way will work better than another. As you progress on your journey, you may choose to work with different ones. I have by no means included all the many types of meditations you can use. The most important thing to recognize is there is not a wrong way, and it is critical to be kind to yourself during this process of figuring out which practice works for you in this moment.

Meditation has been scientifically proven to change body chemistry, reduce stress, effectively alter emotions and reactions, and bring your body and mind to a state of peace. There is no need to meditate for hours a day, as some hold as a preconceived notion to see change. Even if you take ten minutes a day to remove all the distractions and claim the time for yourself to simply "be," you will see results. Social media, phones, noise, music, television, and so many other distractions surround us and stop us from truly being in the present moment. Meditation is about accessing that present moment and checking in with yourself. If thoughts come up, they are not to be judged but recognized. I have heard several sources recommend that if challenging thoughts come up while meditating, you should notice them and visualize them floating away on clouds, so you can be brought back to the present moment.

Different Types of Meditation

Energetic Meditation

There are several ways to feel energy. Bring the energy in as you learned in the previous chapter and allow that energy to wash over you. Feel the energy in your body, and allow it to visit different parts of your body. This connection to your energy body is relaxing. It also affirms to your soul that you know you are more than the constant barrage of thoughts in your head. When you are in this state of relaxation, feeling your energy flow, it brings you to the present moment, which is what meditation is all about. In this state, you might achieve a deep relaxation or find yourself receiving answers and guidance.

Guided Meditation

When I first began meditating, this was the only way I could do it. There are countless people who offer guided meditations on CDs, apps, or on youtube.com. When listening to one, you simply close your eyes and follow the instructions. It is like a story you are being slowly drawn into. Sometimes this is the easiest way to "calm the monkey mind" so you have something or someone to focus on. Some of my favorite guided meditations are the Silva System and hypnotic meditations.

The Silva System (www.silvalifesystem.com; you can visit the site for access to free meditations), developed by Jose Silva in the 1960s, is an effective way of training the mind to relax. Several celebrities, athletes, and speakers have sworn by the Silva System as a way to reduce stress, eliminate illness, tap into intuitive guidance, and truly create the life desired. The 25-minute free-guided meditation trains you so that you won't need it after a while. It is a method to bring in to your life quickly, any time you feel stressed, to change your emotional and physical states.

Hypnotic Meditation

These meditations, as offered by Dr. Steve G. Jones and others, are often helpful. Dr. Jones is a gifted hypnotherapist who offers meditations that are hypnotic journeys. You can look him up on youtube.com or look up "hypnotic meditations" on Google to find thousands to choose from. These can be handy for achieving whatever it is you would like: reducing stress, stopping smoking, finding motivation, achieving wealth, and so much more. There is no shortage of free guided and hypnotic meditations on the Internet or you can research online and buy CDs. Your local library might even have some to borrow. The most important aspect of finding a guided or hypnotic meditation is to find someone who has a voice you like to listen to and find relaxing.

Sensory Meditation

These are among my favorite as they are simple to do, and you can truly do them anywhere. There is always so much going on around us, and we are only aware of a small percentage at a time. To do a sensory meditation, sit in a place in your home or outside. Tune into one sense. I enjoy the auditory version most, but any sense is applicable. When you tune into your auditory sense, you close your eyes and just "hear." First, if you are outside, you might notice the hum of traffic in the distance, perhaps a few birds or the wind. As you continue to listen, you will recognize the many other sounds around you. Sensory meditations are relaxing and make you realize how much you experience in each and every moment, many of which are typically not consciously recognized.

Mantra Meditation

As you learned in the Affirmations chapter, it is powerful to affirm what you want. In a mantra meditation, you find a quiet space and repeat over and over either a sentence, a mantra/chant/affirmation (as found in the chakra chapters), or a few sentences that affirm what you want in your life. I have found "I AM" statements the most powerful. You can also write your own for aspects that you want to experience more often in your life. When you repeat these mantras, either out loud or in your mind, you tell your subconscious what you want. As you repeat them, you can let your mind go and get into a quiet space. Your brain will know to repeat them, and sometimes you will feel your body relax into them. An example of a mantra would be one of my favorites: "I am limitless, I am unlimited, there are no limits to what I can create."

Walking in Nature

I grew up in New York City where it is beyond challenging to find a quiet place. Yet, as I think back, I was always drawn to the East River or Central Park, which were both a few blocks from where I grew up. Even if you are in a city, there is always a place to see some grass and experience nature. Nature is healing. You can learn a lot from watching animals and connecting with plants and trees. Nature is truly about flow and the current moment. A walk in nature or sitting and taking in everything around you, truly taking it in and noticing, is about as meditative as it gets. If you can be by water, that is also wonderful; listen to the sounds of it, close your eyes, and experience the beauty around you.

Cycling Meditation

I learned about cycling meditations from the book, *The Energy Cure*, by William Bengston and Sylvia Fraser (Sounds True, 2010). Dr. Bengston had huge success in curing cancer patients by using this technique. I include a part of the method here that I have found hugely effective. The complete technique is explained in the book and is a powerful energy healing methodology that anyone can learn. It is a simple method that requires practice but is one that brings such joy and allows rising to a high vibration. It is not surprising that it can elevate your mood and invigorate your body so rapidly.

To do a cycling meditation, list twenty things that you want or desire. These are not things such as world peace; these are things for you or things you want to be. For example, a new car, a loving relationship, a new kitchen, a two-week vacation, to be more confident, to speak another language, etc. Select things that are just for you and that you know will bring you happiness upon receiving them. Once you have your list, think of a picture that represents each one. Now, close your eyes and go through that list in your head, over and over and over. Be sure to picture those things that will bring you joy. Cycling these images faster and faster requires practice but is worth the time. Doing this repeatedly will bring you to a state of calmness and joy and create a very high vibrational energy.

Exercise 20: Meditating to Bring You to the Present Moment

I would like you to pick two types of meditation and try them each once. (Of course you can try them more than once or more than two types of meditations if you like.) In preparation for each meditation exercise you choose, sit comfortably. Allow yourself time to be still and turn off your phone. Watch your breathing or count your breath in, holding it, and letting it out. Some practices suggest starting with the count of breathing in for four, holding for four, and letting out for eight. You can play with these numbers and find the ones that are right and comfortable with your own breathing patterns. You can also simply notice your breathing. If you find you breathe very rapidly, take a few moments to slow it down. Do this without strain or causing yourself stress. Notice if you sit for a few minutes and watch your breath and allow yourself to be present, your breath will probably slow naturally on its own. Write down how you felt after each meditation exercise.

ANCHORS

"All you need is one safe anchor to keep you grounded when the rest of your life spins out of control."

—KATIE KACVINSKY, *AWAKEN*

We all have plenty of moments we can recall that bring back strong emotions. Unfortunately, the common habit is to concentrate on the ones that cause us to experience the less than happy emotions. By now, you have learned that where you put your attention is what you put out there to the Universe and create. An anchor taps into a moment that brings you such joy and happiness and switches your emotions when you find yourself in a state of mind you do not want to be in.

An anchor should be a moment where you felt nothing but total joy and appreciation. The more you can visualize that moment and bring all your senses in, the better. Your anchor could be a recent moment or a moment that stands out from your past, a moment in time when you felt alive, joyful, and deep happiness from within. Something powerful—maybe a time when you had belly laughs with friends, a time someone showed you great appreciation, a moment when you were being honored, or a moment where you felt deep peace, as a walk in the woods will sometimes grant you. The point is that when you think of this moment all you feel is joy, love, and happiness.

I remember watching the news when I was young and the first story was always a horrific one. Daily, we are shown and told horror stories of what is wrong with the world. It can become overwhelming. Between this and our own third-dimension challenges, it can be difficult to feel empowered or concentrate on the positive moments. "Attention Shifting" in Section I and "Gratitude" in Section III showed how powerful shifting our energy to the positive aspects of life can be. This can be done in a moment of recalling something precious or happy. Discovering and using an anchor magnifies that feeling of happiness as it is a moment so powerful, it can take you to another space in a few minutes, once you learn how to tune into it and feel the magic of it. An anchor can truly turn a frown or heavy negative state into a happy and elated state of mind in a matter of minutes.

An anchor is helpful in remembering and bringing forth, into your present state of consciousness, a moment where you felt pure joy. It is a reminder to yourself how good life can be. Recalling an anchoring moment in a time of stress or a time when you feel stuck is a wonderful way to press a reset button on that moment. We can all get stuck in our own heads and stories. You have learned ways to bring yourself to the present moment and how in that moment, you can decide how you want to feel next. An anchor is a powerful way to switch that story and remind yourself that life can be wonderful. You have felt that joy and happiness before, and you will surely feel it again.

You can use an anchor in different scenarios and see when you are able to utilize it best to switch your mood. You can use it before a meeting that you are nervous about, as a means of gaining confidence and joy. You can use an anchor in a moment when you feel stressed out and helpless about a situation. You can use an anchor if you are mad about something, as a way to help calm yourself and remind yourself of the goodness in the world and in your life. You can use an anchor first thing in the morning to start the day off right or before bed, so you can go to sleep with a smile on your face. Any time is an appropriate time to use an anchor; you just need to remember that you have the power to do so at any time!

Exercise 21: Anchoring Yourself to the Present Moment and Joy

Now it is time for you to come up with that anchoring moment before you take the next step. Imagine a time when you felt your heart leaping with joy; a time when you felt tears of gratitude or happiness. Not only should you recall that moment, but when you have one, sit with it. Imagine the people who were there and your feelings for them; see them and the situation, feel the emotions of it. If you can recall a smell or taste, bring that back too as well as any visual cues. The more sensory awareness you can recall, the more powerful your anchor will be. Sit with this for a few minutes with your eyes closed and a smile on your face. Bring in that emotion as if you were truly revisiting it now in this moment. If you like, you can do Exercise 19 "Feeling Energy in Your Body and Using it to Heal Yourself" before you bring in the anchor.

Write down the anchor and what your experience was like bringing it back to the present. Choose a moment in the next few days when you will use that anchor at least once in different scenarios. Consider beginning or ending the day with the anchor. Think about your anchor when you are stuck in traffic, annoyed at work, or when you're about to engage in a challenging conversation. By thinking about the moments when you will use your anchor, the anchor will come to mind in those times. After you have used your anchor at that appropriate time, write about your experience. Describe how it helped to change your mood and emotions at that moment.

HIGHER SELF

"The soul always knows what to do to heal itself. The challenge is to silence the mind."

—CAROLINE MYSS

We are so much more than our bodies. We have access to unlimited information through our Higher Self/soul at all times. However, we are usually too wrapped up in our daily human experience to recognize it. There is great power in tapping into our soul and getting to know ourselves at that level. We can release the limitations our human selves have put on us. Soul realizations can help us shed limiting beliefs and move forward with confidence. In getting to know our soul, we come to know we are not alone, and we can be grateful for this moment, where we can access our Higher Self and receive that feeling of love and self-acceptance. Our soul is never judging us; it recognizes that this life is a journey, and we always do the best we can. In tapping into our soul and participating in regular conversations with our Higher Self, we can transform any feelings of loneliness or self-doubt that we have had and can move in to a place of unlimited power and connectivity.

I once met a shaman, Lench Archuletta, who had our group do an exercise where he asked us to point to ourselves. Take this second and point to yourself and see where your hand is without thinking about it before you read on. I was in a group of about fifty people at the time and forty-nine of those people pointed to their hearts (one person pointed to their head). Shaman Lench looked at that one person perplexed; from what you have learned so far, you can see that person was someone more in their head than in their heart at the time. We know intuitively there is much more to "us" than the cells and bones that create our genetic makeup, but we are not given tools to access that part. We are told to work on our brains, to train them, keep them fresh, and to always learn. That is valuable. We are told to eat right, exercise, and look after our physical body, which is also powerful and important. However, I feel it is just as important, if not more important, to do the inner work that connects us to our soul/Higher Self. Remember, we are made of body, mind, *and* spirit! Our spirit is that aspect of ourselves that is our true selves and is non-judging and perfect.

You have already done exercises to shed the limiting beliefs and patterns that had you feeling like you were truly a victim to your own mind. You know now that your mind is helpful. Yet you have much more powerful tools within you: your heart and soul. To get in touch with your soul, you need to turn off distractions and look within. You will need to quiet the cell phones, television, computers, and everything else that distracts you and let your inner self know that you want to hear what it is feeling. Through meditation, you can access your soul self. However, sometimes you still might have trouble discerning where that inner guidance is coming from. You may doubt whether or not it is your brain or heart and how in the world you can tell the difference. There are a few ways in which you can differentiate between the two.

Your soul will never give you guidance that leaves you feeling defeated. Your soul knows you are all powerful and have the ability to tap into unlimited knowledge. You might get so caught up in the way things were and the patterns you have created that sometimes it becomes hard to see that there is another way out of a situation. Accessing your soul is a powerful means to get out of your own way and follow what is in flow and what is the path of least resistance. I have found several helpful ways to contact your Higher Self and ensure the guidance you seek is coming from there. I will offer a couple of exercises to choose from. I also encourage you to try other methods such as the previously laid out meditation practices. These techniques will help you to quiet your mind and allow you to receive guidance from your Higher Self/ Your Soul.

~~~~~~~~~~~~~~~~~~~~~~~~~~~~~~~~~~~~

Exercise 22: Connecting to Your Higher Self (Soul) to Receive Guidance

Read through both exercises and see which one appeals to you. Try one or both and write your thoughts down afterward.

Automatic Writing

Think of two questions you want answers to or guidance on; a place in your life where you have felt stuck or can feel a pattern is in place but just can't seem to wrap your head around finding a way out of it. Write the questions down so they are concretely in your mind.

Get in a quiet place. Make sure you have pen and paper or your computer set to a program where you can type. Make sure phones are turned off and you have at least a few minutes. Take some time to center yourself. You can use Exercise 19 "Feeling Energy in Your Body and Using it to Heal Yourself" or just take some deep breaths. I would also like you to have a timer handy. You will ask yourself the first question, and set your timer for ninety seconds. Without "thinking" ahead of time, freely write the answers as they come. Do not worry about correcting typos, and do not judge yourself as you write. Simply write and see what comes. When the timer goes off, set the timer again, write your second question, and write your answers. Again, no judging, no editing, no getting in your head; just let it flow. After you are done, reread what you wrote and see if any new insights come to you. See if you tapped into an idea or solution that you never thought of before.

When you quiet and center yourself, have an intention to figure an issue out, and set time aside to do it, you'll be amazed at what comes to you. It is the opposite of sitting and worrying about something. Rather, you ask your Higher Self, in that centered and present moment, to help you reach the inner guidance that is always there for you.

Pendulum

Make sure you set aside ten to fifteen minutes to try this exercise. Turn your phone off and get into a quiet space. Take some breaths, center yourself, and then move forward with the exercise.

If you do not own a pendulum, use a necklace with some form of pendant, charm, or crystal for this exercise. For ease of writing and understanding, I will call that part of the necklace the pendant. If you use a necklace, hold it so the two parts of the chain are together and the pendant hangs down. Hold the chain an inch or two down between your thumb and pointer finger and let the pendant hang free. Secure your elbow on a flat surface so that you know your arm is in a steady position. The first thing you will ask the pendulum (it may seem as if you are talking to a necklace or pendulum, but you are actually accessing your Higher Self) is, "Pendulum, show me 'yes.'" The pendulum should begin to swing on its own either sideways, back to front, or perhaps in circles. If you do not get results or the pendulum barely moves, try saying, "Pendulum bigger." You can also hold your other hand under the pendant, which generates more energy. Next you will ask the pendulum to "Stop." You will then ask the pendulum to show you "no." This will be a different motion. If the pendulum went back and forth for yes, it might go in circles for no. If it went side to side, it now might go back to forth. Take a few minutes and work with this. Remember, you can say, "bigger" and you can put your other hand underneath the pendant. This will help to generate more energy.

Most people are shocked when they do this. They know they are not moving the object themselves, yet the pendulum moves. Now that the pendulum moves, you can ask any yes or no question. You might start with easy ones such as "Is my name John?" to see for yourself this does in fact work. When you are comfortable, move on to other questions. You can ask the pendulum to stop in between questions to ensure that you get a clear answer for each question. Many doubting and disbelieving clients and friends have had their jaws drop open when using a pendulum for the first time. There is no denying it is giving you answers and you are not cognitively swinging it. It is simply a matter of being in a relaxed state and using this tool to gain answers. This allows your Higher Self to step in and give you the guidance you require. Write down the answers you received during this exercise. Know that next time you use the pendulum you will again have to ask it to show you "yes" or "no" because they can change. If you resonate with using the pendulum, you can buy one and have it attuned to you with a simple meditation and energy exercise; you can look up exercises online to do this so you will not have to go through the "show me yes or no" process each time.

If you have the time, try both of these exercises to determine which one works better for you. There are certain times I feel guided to use one over the other. There is no wrong or right, it is all about what feels comfortable and resonates with you. I must admit that I felt pretty silly using the pendulum at first. However, it has given me unmistakable guidance time and time again. It is a tool to come back to often when you need guidance or a connection; the same can be said of automatic writing.

LOVE AND CONNECTIVITY
(Oneness)

"Love recognizes no barriers. It jumps hurdles, leaps fences, penetrates walls to arrive at its destination full of hope."

——MAYA ANGELOU

Millions of songs, poems, books, letters, and quotes have been written on the subject of love. You can probably quote ten phrases on love in a few seconds: "Love is all there is," "All you need is love," and "Love thy neighbor," to name a few. We all know this word; we all have experienced it, in one form or another either as a parent, relative, child, sibling, friend, or with a pet. But we may not fully grasp what love is and how it connects us all. Love is the most powerful of all emotions because it connects us all; it defies judgment, and it brings us to the beautiful space of appreciating each other.

We can easily pull up that feeling of love when we think of someone who makes us happy. But can you pull up that feeling of love for someone you feel has made you unhappy? It speaks to the Deepak quote that we all do the best we can from our own state of consciousness. It relates to Exercise 1 "Learning to Forgive Yourself and Others with Ho'oponopono" where we forgive ourselves for the judgment we put on others and ourselves. We all are connected and deserve love. After reading that last sentence, if you have thoughts in your head such as, "Well I can think of one person who doesn't deserve love," that is the person that probably needs it the most.

In my private practice, the majority of clients who have experienced challenging, combative, and aggressive relationships with their mothers as children have also had a difficult time coming to terms with love and its place in their lives. We are taught the mother relationship is the first nurturing relationship we have and when this is not in place, there can be a challenge for that child to feel loved. This, in turn, can manifest itself in a lack of self-love and dissatisfying relationships with others. In healing and dealing with those emotions and coming to a place of inner love, we can change the love we feel for everyone and everything around us. I have also had clients who had the same experiences of an abusive mother work to heal the issue and experience deep connecting relationships.

You can live a happy life whether your childhood was happy or challenging. You need to look at some of these patterns, as you have done throughout this book, and eliminate the ones that do not serve you and the ones that limit not only how you see yourself but how you view others as well. I love the Dr. Jill Bolte Taylor quote, "Just like children, emotions heal when they are heard and validated." Healing those feelings of any lack of self-love puts us in a good place to receive and feel the love and connectivity we have with each and every other living thing on this planet.

I highly recommend either reading Dr. Jill Bolte Taylor's book, *Stroke of Insight*, or looking up her video TED Talk. The video is twenty minutes long and life changing. Dr. Taylor is a neuro-scientist who witnessed herself having a stroke. The left side of her brain was affected, so her speech and logical thinking became more and more impaired. At that time, her focus was on the right side of her brain, which controls connectivity and love, as well as our spiritual nature. Dr. Taylor was shown how connected we all are during the process. She truly experienced "Love is all there is" and within her twenty minutes of sharing her experience, you can glimpse what that feels like.

When we feel love, we feel connected. We feel light, happy, joyful, and have a deep sense that everything will be okay. We feel complete, satisfied, and present. There is no judgment, just those strong and overwhelming emotions of positivity and warmth. This, believe it or not, is our natural state and one that connects us. Within the true us, our soul never feels anything less. There-fore, the more you connect with your soul, the true you, the more you can bring this feeling into your daily life.

It is so easy to share love and make someone else happy. A sim-ple gesture can brighten someone's day, which can inspire them to turn around and brighten the next person's day. Perhaps it's a smile to a person on the sidewalk or in a store, or a kind word of gratitude to let someone know you care. It could be a note or email to some-one letting them know you appreciate them. All of these actions stimulate that loving feeling in us for others, and you will be amazed that when you make this a part of your daily life, how much more love you feel on a regular basis.

Love is non-judgment. We all have our stuff. We all do the best we can in this moment. Most of us struggle with self-love. Most of us hold on to some kind of anger for someone else or a feeling of how unfair a situation is. But that is judgment. Everything that has happened thus far in your life has gotten you to this moment, and all of that is to be loved. My illness was the most challenging time of my life. Without it, I don't know if I would have become a healing practitioner. Without this experience, I might not have had the deep empathy for my clients when they told me how challenging it was to be sick and in doctors' offices undergoing numerous invasive tests and diagnoses. Everything is perfect and has happened for us to experience, learn from, and grow from. Loving and coming to terms with your past and the people in it is an important step in freeing yourself to feel love in the highest frequency possible.

On the next pages are two exercises to do for love. One is for you to feel that connectivity to everyone and everything else. The other is an action for you to take to share the love you have generated. I can tell you that love is indeed the answer, and the more you align yourself with love, the more you can create and experience life here as Heaven on Earth.

Exercise 23: Loving and Honoring
Our Connection to All

Feeling Love and Connection to All Things

I would like you to take a minute and get yourself centered. Turn off all devices and make sure you have at least ten minutes of quiet time. Read this through once before doing the exercise. When you are in a quiet space, sit down with your feet on the floor, close your eyes, and begin Exercise 19 "Feeling Energy in Your Body and Using it to Heal Yourself" to feel the energy in your hands. When you feel the energy nice and strong, pull that energy up through your hands, up your arms, and into your heart. If you have a challenging time with this, place a hand on your heart and see if you can feel the energy in your heart this way.

Next, sit with that energy in your heart and think of someone or something you love tremendously. Imagine that energy bubble growing with the love, and picture it as a big ball of white light glowing in your heart. When you feel it strongly there, let that white energy bubble of light get bigger and bigger. See it expanding to cover your body. Visualize it getting as big as the room you are in. See it grow to surround the building you are in or the area you are in outside. Watch it grow, and feel that love. Watch it reaching out as big as the town you are in. See it touching the people and encompassing all the people in the town, the plants, and the animals. Feel that love and the expansion of the bubble, and let it sit in each space as it grows and then you pour that love into it.

Watch the love bubble expanding to your state, your country, all the while thinking about the things you love about each. Maybe it is the weather and the joy that being with friends brings. Perhaps it is your favorite local restaurant. Maybe it is the nature around you or a local park. Whatever it is, let that love bubble grow. See it expand beyond your country, to the continent, and eventually to cover the entire planet. Feel the love you have and that we all have for being able to experience this humanness and the feeling of love. Next, imagine this love bubble reaching out into space; feel gratitude for the sun, moon, planets, stars, and for the whole vast Universe. When the bubble is as large as you can visualize, sit in that space for a few minutes. Feel all the love you have and imagine that love with the billions of people on this planet, and with the billions of trees, animals, stars, and the abundance all around us. There is so much love on this planet and in this Universe.

When you are ready, pull that love back in and feel the gratitude the planet gives you for sending out that love. You might feel it in people you pictured and in knowing how they feel about you. You might feel it in your pet and how they look forward to cuddles from you each day. Whatever makes you feel that love and connection, allow that to continue to deflate the bubble into you knowing you receive that love tenfold. When you feel the bubble reach the size of your heart again, relax here and take a few breaths. When you are ready, open your eyes.

Take a moment to write about this experience.

Showing Love to Others

Today or within the next few days, show love to someone in any of the ways below or in your own way.

- Smile at someone in the grocery store or while walking.
- Let someone ahead of you in a store line or while driving.
- Write a note of appreciation or love to someone you care about.
- Do an errand or extend a kind gesture to someone you care about or someone in your community.
- Call someone and tell them you love, care, and appreciate them.
- Find out how you can volunteer in your community.

If you come up with some other way to express your love with someone else, that is wonderful too. After you do this action, write down the person's reaction and how you felt doing this for someone.

SECTION III
CONSIDERATIONS

Section III offered many ways to bring yourself to and stay in the present moment (if only for a little while). The more you call yourself into the present moment, by these and other exercises, the more life will flow. You can see how you affect your current reality. You recognize how being present allows for the opportunity to change where your attention goes and how you react.

All of the exercises in this section allowed you to get still and tap into that magical moment of presence and all it offers. Play with these different exercises. Some are so simple you can keep them as a daily or weekly practice. Know that the more you call yourself to the present moment, the more of a habit it will become. I cannot overstate the importance of the gratitude exercises and of feeling self-love. These emotions create magic and call the lives of your dreams to you. Practicing meditating or connecting to your Higher Self are powerful messages you send affirming that you want to feel that connection and receive guidance. Have fun, play, and explore the exercises as you see fit. Remember how it felt doing the exercises and how wonderful it feels to be present! Section IV guides you through some new ways of thought and offers tools to help you on your journey to stay present. There are common challenges you might face on your path to transformation and the exercises in the next section will help you stay on your path to walk right on through them.

SECTION IV
Discovering New Ways
of Thought and Tools to Help

"Feelings or emotions are the universal language and are to be honored. They are authentic expressions of who you are at your deepest place."

—JUDITH WRIGHT

I trust by now you have felt some shifts in your mental and emotional being and have connected a little deeper with your soul, the true you. You have learned how to tap into the present moment, understand the messages from your energy body, and the challenges and patterns from your past. I applaud you for making it this far and moving past the resistance that arose as you faced some of those old patterns and beliefs. I hope you have given yourself sufficient gratitude for being willing to transform. Know that your soul thanks you and is appreciative that you are taking this initiative to become your best self.

As you move forward on this journey, it is helpful to acquire tools and take notice of when you have perceived setbacks. You are human, still on this planet. While you are here, you will have times that challenge you. You will have experiences in which it seems all you have learned appears to have gone out the window (at least temporarily). That "temporarily" is the key. Know that you have the tools to make the changes lasting. The state of un-wellness or challenge is to be noticed and affirmed that "this too shall pass." Be kind to yourself and know that every experience is one you learn from. It is not just the experiences you deem good that have something to offer. Often it is the challenging ones that offer the greatest blessings in disguise. It is important to notice when you experience a challenging and emotional time. However, you must avoid becoming stuck in them for months on end and you must give yourself credit for moving forward.

Emotions are meant to be honored, as Judith Wright's quote states. This section gives tools that will allow you to move past those moments that might seem challenging, to make peace with some of your human-ness and difficulties, and to show you how to move forward with the confidence that life can and will be different beginning right now.

LETTING GO AND RECEIVING

"What you seek is seeking you."

—RUMI

Understanding why "letting go" is so powerful makes it much easier to apply in your life. You have learned how to become present. In this section you will learn the importance of setting goals and how to begin to manifest your desires. The greatest hurdle I have come across in manifesting things for myself and with my clients is a holding on too tightly to how we want things to go and putting a specific timeline on when. When you cling to what you want and how and when you want it, you send out two signals: First, you do not trust it will be given to you, and second, you know best how the Universe can deliver and which timing is best. When you cling to thinking that you know best, that is the ego and that is living from fear instead of trust and love. You can actually block the request from manifesting because you cling so tightly to your exact vision of how it needs to happen. This can cause you to miss signs that your request is in fact on its way to you, perhaps differently than you pictured. The tighter you cling to these things, the bigger the lesson will tell you that you do not always know what is best! Learn how to let go and be ready to receive the magic the Universe can so readily deliver.

I separated from my husband a few years ago and am grateful we are able to be friends and am forever grateful for him for helping me bring our two children into this world. I hesitated to get into another relationship and spent a few years dating. As I dated and from hindsight from my marriage, past relationships, and all the changes I made in myself, I made a list of things I wanted in a partner. It was written in positive statements and began with "He is…" My friends would joke about my list, and I thought no one person could possibly fill all of the two pages of requirements. But as a fun kind of dreamy exercise, I would still add to my list when something occurred to me. I wasn't looking at it every day or even every month. I wasn't wishing this man would walk into my life now. I just let the Universe know I knew what I wanted and what would make me happy.

Last spring I decided it would be wonderful to have someone to be with and do things with. I told the Universe I had my book to write so, "Nothing too serious please!" In walked a man who was every single thing on my list. The funny thing was I watched myself struggle to accept this gift from the Universe into my life. "I said not now, Universe." "He can't possibly have all the qualities he seems to have." "Maybe I don't deserve all of this goodness." "I have a book to write." It is so interesting how our ego tries to take us backward into what is known as safe and does not allow us to simply relax and receive.

When I did say, "Hmm, maybe the Universe is smarter than me," I got out my list. I recognized this man was every single thing I had requested. I also recognized that while my book was not yet finished, this man had come into my life at one of the toughest times: as my stepfather, a man who had been in my life for thirty-five years, struggled for life. This amazing man had been through hospital visits and the pain of an illness with his own father and was beyond supportive of me. It was a time when I could have resorted to my old behavior, said any number of excuses, and not allowed myself to receive this gift. Instead, I allowed myself to open up and receive a gift that grows in beauty every single day I am with him, and I know with absolute confidence will continue to blossom.

When you put your order in with the Universe and get very clear on what you want, you do the first part in receiving. In letting go and not obsessing about how or when but trusting the Universe to provide when the opportunity is perfect for you, you do the second part: set yourself up for receiving. I find the underlying key ingredients to receiving are also self-love and being present, discussed in Section III; believing you are worthy of whatever you asked for and noticing when it appears.

I love the classic story of the man in a flood: A terrible storm came into a town and local officials sent out an emergency warning that the riverbanks would soon overflow and flood the nearby homes. They ordered everyone in the town to evacuate immediately.

A faithful Christian man heard the warning and decided to stay, saying to himself, "I will trust God and if I am in danger, then

God will send a Divine miracle to save me." The neighbors came by his house and said to him, "We're leaving and there is room for you in our car, please come with us!" But the man declined. "I have faith that God will save me."

As the man stood on his porch watching the water rise up the steps, a man in a canoe paddled by and called to him, "Hurry and come into my canoe, the waters are rising quickly!" But the man again said, "No thanks, God will save me."

The floodwaters rose higher and poured water into his living room and the man had to retreat to the second floor. A police motorboat came by and saw him at the window. "We will come up and rescue you!" they shouted. But the man refused, waving them off saying, "Use your time to save someone else! I have faith that God will save me!"

The flood waters rose higher and higher and the man had to climb up to his rooftop.

A helicopter spotted him and dropped a rope ladder. A rescue officer came down the ladder and pleaded with the man, "Grab my hand and I will pull you up!" But the man still refused, folding his arms tightly to his body. "No thank you! God will save me!"

Shortly after, the house broke up and the floodwaters swept the man away and he drowned.

When in Heaven, the man stood before God and asked, "I put all of my faith in You. Why didn't You come and save me?" And God said, "Son, I sent you a warning. I sent you a car. I sent you a canoe. I sent you a motorboat. I sent you a helicopter. What more were you looking for?"

This is a classic example of someone who asked for something (help), and knew what he wanted but wasn't present enough to see the help right in front of him. Help or whatever you ask for might not come in the exact way, package, or timing you imagined. Give the Universe some wiggle room and also give yourself enough love and presence to know when you are given a gift. Open yourself up to receiving by knowing you are worthy of whatever it is you ask for: more money, a healthy relationship, a new job, your own health and well-being, a car or home you would be proud of, friends that inspire you. Whatever it is—know it can be yours. Take the first step by getting very clear on what you want, relax, and know it will come in!

~~~~~~

Exercise 24: Letting Go and Receiving

Think of something you want to receive such as a new job, car, electronics, house, or a new relationship. So many times I see clients put limits on what they think they can receive and in doing so they tell themselves they truly believe they don't deserve more. In this exercise, I want to tell you the sky is the limit—beyond the sky if you can imagine that far, just as I did not feel it was possible for one person to have all the attributes on my list and was proven wrong. Let your mind go wild a bit and then do the following four-step process.

1. Claim what you want; go into detail and list them all in positive form. If it is a job, highlight your abilities,

don't limit yourself by thinking "there is no perfect job out there for me." An example is if you are looking for a job with certain aspects: "I would like a job that allows me to showcase my way of coming up with new ideas, highlights my ability to get along with people, lets me have a flexible schedule so I can be present for my kids if need be." Remember the only limits are the ones you create. Write down at least seven aspects for what you request and remember to keep them in positive form.

2. As you have learned from past exercises, the more you bring all your senses the more powerful your experience will be. Really let yourself get into that feeling state of imaging that all of the things on your list have been met. Remember to not think about the how or the when.

3. Affirm to yourself that you love yourself and are worthy. Affirm that you are ready to receive the object of your desire whenever the Universe knows is the perfect timing and in whatever form it will come in.

4. Thank the Universe for receiving your request and thank yourself for taking the time to make this conscious decision to declare what you want!

Write down how this exercise felt for you. Remember, your list is your own—edit it at will. Over the two years it took to "perfect my list for a partner," I added and deleted things, recognizing that as I was changing, my needs and wants were changing too. No one will judge you on this request; by revisiting it but not harping on it obsessively you let the Universe know it is important to you but you also trust that it will be provided when the time is right. Know also that this does not mean sitting on your couch waiting for it to appear. If you are looking for a job, check those want ads, if you are looking for a mate, ask a friend or co-worker if they know anyone you might be compatible with or join a dating site. Take some sort of movement or step so the Universe knows you are serious and then stand back and know you are worthy of receiving what the Universe will offer!

EMBRACING YOUR SHADOWS

"There is no coming to consciousness without pain. People will do anything, no matter how absurd, in order to avoid facing their own soul. One does not become enlightened by imagining figures of light, but by making the darkness conscious."

—CARL JUNG

Humans are self-deprecating creatures. You can gain much strength by recognizing your own "shadow" characteristics. By examining and understanding them, you can come to a kind of peace with them. You can understand how they have served you so far, and how you can use them to help and not hinder your future progress. This is a time to recognize that as humans you have many different characteristics, and each has a purpose in your life.

I have always known I was someone who had verrrrry little patience. It was something I was not proud of. In recognizing it as a "shadow," I realized it also translated to myself more than it did with situations and other people. But my lack of patience is also what caused me to take action. I felt in many situations, "Well if I don't go ahead and do it, no one else will; I guess I will be the one to get it done." This has served me well countless times. I now use that lack of patience as an asset when I can, instead of insulting myself because of it. It works…most of the time.

I ask you to tap into your own patience and self-love with yourself as you go along the process of discovering your shadows, whether they be impatience, anger, losing your temper, worrying, a tendency to lie, addiction, anxiety, depression, or whatever they may be. In discovering these shadows, you do not dwell on "what is bad in you." Rather, you locate an emotion or coping mechanism, come to terms with it, and see how it has served to help you in the past. Then you do not allow yourself to be victimized by it in the future.

Before I knew my shadow was impatience, I was a victim to it. I felt it getting the best of me. My biggest lack of patience was within myself and toward myself, always criticizing myself for not getting enough done and becoming a perfectionist. When something wasn't happening fast enough, or when I waited for someone who was late, I felt myself get frustrated inside, sometimes even to the point of getting a stomachache. In knowing, "Yup, patience is a challenge for me," I can look at the situation from a truthful and objective view rather than letting my subjectivity and lack of patience take over. It doesn't mean I don't get annoyed if someone is very late, but it does mean that I know it is me reacting to it because of me, not because of them.

Knowing my shadow of impatience has also proved helpful in situations where things are not happening fast enough for me. I can step back and look at the situation and assess it differently. The previous chapter, "Letting Go and Receiving," emphasized the importance of not putting your human timetable on what you want. Yet, I felt myself frequently getting wound up when things were not happening fast enough for my liking. Knowing my shadow, I'd look at it objectively and say, "Okay, either I accept this is perfect timing or do something about it to make it happen quicker." Depending on the situation, sometimes I would step up knowing an action would facilitate movement. Other times, I could just step back and say, "Okay Universe, I might not agree on the timing of this right now, but I am going to assume you know better than I do!"

Knowing our shadows is also important because of how hard we can be on ourselves. No one can be smiley and their most positive uplifting selves a hundred percent of the time. Life happens, and your emotions are coping mechanisms and signals that show you how you feel and what you can do about it. All your emotions are to be honored, as Judith Wright's quote states at the beginning of this section. All of our emotions make you who you are, all are a part of the nature of the beautiful human, you! The more you look at your shadows and not judge them or berate yourself for them, the better off you (and the people around you) will be. It is of far greater value to understand and appreciate how your shadows have served you.

It is important in recognizing your shadows that you pay them gratitude for how they helped you and still serve you. When you don't acknowledge them, they lead you and can come out in harmful ways to yourself and those around you. In paying them gratitude and recognizing why they have been there and what good they have done for you, you celebrate part of yourself. You shine light on what you might have always labeled as a negative aspect of yourself. One that you might have thought you had no control of. In this process, you can fall in love with yourself a little more. You can recognize your humanness, forgive yourself, and accept a part of yourself that was "dark" before this illumination.

In bringing your shadows to light, you free yourself from that darkness. It only takes a little light to see in front of you to destroy the blackness. The exercise that follows will help you bring a shadow to light and embrace it. Be kind to yourself in this process, as the shadows arise. Remember, you might have been using this as a coping mechanism or defense for years, perhaps decades or longer. It is okay, and you are perfect just the way you are. By being present, as you have learned how to do, and by noticing these shadows, you now have power over them and can use them to your advantage instead of using them as a reaction. There is huge power in doing so!

~~~~~~~~~~~~~~~~~~~~~~~~~~~~~~~~

Exercise 25: Shining Light on Your Shadow

I would like you to think of an aspect of yourself you think of as "negative" or that you did not like about yourself. The following are some common shadows: anger, impatience, lying, anxiety, worrying, jealousy, addictions, being overpowering and controlling, short tempered, fear, overworking, overeating, and procrastination.

When you have this one "shadow" in mind, get yourself comfortable, take a few slow breaths, and proceed.

Put your hand on your heart and tell yourself it is "okay" that you have this shadow. Tell yourself you are grateful, and you are brave enough to face it head on.

Ask yourself how has this shadow served you in your life.

For example, if your shadow is anger: Maybe you have found yourself angry in situations and people have reacted quickly to you because they were afraid of your increased anger. But as a result, it helped to get things done speedier. If you felt anxiety at times, maybe it has served you by helping you feel safe and secure; it kept you from trying things you were not comfortable with. If you have an addictive personality, maybe you needed to use those addictions at some point to "numb out" and not face the emotions or a truly challenging situation you were afraid of, and perhaps did not have the tools to deal with at that time. Your shadows have served you in some way, at some point in time, otherwise you would not have continued to use them.

As you come up with the ways in which your shadow has helped you, allow yourself to smile and come to peace with it. This is a valuable aspect of the "true" you, and we work on loving every part of ourselves. Know it is okay— everyone has shadows. Shine some light on your own shadow, recognize that you see it but refuse to be a victim of it.

Now, still with your hand on your heart, come up with a scenario where you might see your shadow come up again.

Ask yourself how you can use this shadow without being victimized by it. Think about the proper place for this shadow in your life, and where you would like to take control of it and not be a victim to it anymore. Has this shadow served its purpose and are you ready to move on or can you see this shadow still helping you through parts of your life when it is put in its proper place? When you clearly see your shadow, and work out the emotions around it, you can see it when it comes up or even before it comes up. At that point, you decide how you will use it in the present moment. Remember, being present offers you the ability to see your shadow when it comes up, recognize it, without being reactionary.

Set an intention for how you want to work with your shadow the next time it comes up. Thank yourself for taking the time to recognize it and for getting to know it as well as the emotions tied to it. Know that by doing this, you move powerfully and presently into your future. Write about how it felt to find this shadow, and write your intention of how you intend to deal with it the next time it comes up.

COMMUNITY AND FRIENDS
Asking for Help

"Asking for help does not mean that we are weak or incompetent. It usually indicates an advanced level of honesty and intelligence."

—ANNE WILSON SCHAEF

We all know how wonderful it feels when we are able to help someone. We can easily recall the emotions of love and caring that helping another person brings up in us. Yet, when we are in need or feeling a bit helpless in a situation, we rarely see asking for help as an option. We have been taught that we are all separate and that figuring things out for ourselves is a strength. But I feel this is anything but the truth! If we feel so wonderful when we help people, doesn't it stand to reason that by asking other people for help, we allow them to feel good by helping us? In asking for help, we can see ways out of situations we never would have fathomed. At the same time, we allow for bonding closer to someone, in sharing a common goal. Asking for help is indeed a strength, though a learned one; it is an important lesson for moving forward in life.

It is also powerful to know you are not alone in the circle of people who you know right now; you are part of a bigger community. You are part of the community of your town or city. You are a piece of the community of your state and country. You are a collective among the community of humans; the majority of whom are all connected now so easily by modern technology. You can ask for help in ways you never before imagined, and you can connect with people all over the world. You are no longer limited by the few people who you might know as close friends or family members. You can truly reach out and ask for help for anything that comes up in your life; it is guaranteed you are not the first one to go through it.

I know that before I got sick, I never asked for help. I am a recovering perfectionist, and at the time, my whole attitude was, "I got this." My husband at the time and I had moved into a huge house in New Jersey (more than 5,000 square feet), and I liked things "just so." I was pregnant and then a new mom, but I still wanted to do it all myself. This definitely contributed to me becoming sick. My mind might have felt that I could do it all alone, but my body could not. I would not listen to the signs to slow down, and honestly it never even occurred to me to ask for help. This need to take on everything and control everything was part of what knocked me off of my feet, helped contribute to my diseased state, and led to the chronic pain I suffered with for years. My body had tried to tell me to slow down or ask for help, but in not listening, I gave my body no alternative but to manifest disease so I would have to stop moving.

It does not have to get that bad! You can ask for help before you feel debilitated or as you start to notice, "Hey, maybe I could use a little help here." It is wonderful to see websites such as Go Fund Me and Kickstarter because they back up the idea of asking for help. People have wonderful ideas or goals they want to accomplish but they don't know how they can get the monetary backing. This makes it possible to ask others to help them. It gives the people donating the satisfaction of helping someone else, and it lets the person asking know that they are supported and don't have to do it alone. It is powerful for everyone involved.

One of my arguments for not asking for help was that it was easier if I did it myself. In some cases, this is a valid reason. Yet, if you take the time and patience to explain to someone what you want, it will help. It helps to free you up and grants the other person happiness simultaneously, knowing that they helped. Teaching a child to do dishes or fold laundry, or showing a neighbor how to care for a pet if you need to be away are all worthwhile investments of your time. Helping has the power to benefit all involved and will aide in freeing up your mind and time.

When I lived in New Jersey, I was friends with a lot of mothers who did not have the time to cook every night. For a short while, a couple of us cooked big meals once per week, and we shared them with the other families. It freed us up. The night's we knew we did not have to cook, we could relax knowing we had a home-cooked meal coming for our family. There are ways to collaborate with people in your community that will allow many to benefit.

At some point in time, we all need some kind of help. Getting used to asking is a challenge for some but it helps all parties involved. We live in a world that moves so quickly and demands more and more of us. Helping each other makes life go so much easier, and you get to socialize and validate each other in the process. Maybe you need help with childcare and can swap days with another parent. Perhaps you want to save on gas and can look into carpooling. It might be that you need help managing your bills, going shopping, cooking regular meals, or having someone look after your house when you go away. There are plenty of ways to ask for help where you can possibly trade services, or you can admit you need the extra hands at that time. It is not a weakness but rather a strength to recognize you can use a hand. It will get easier with time, I promise. In the meantime, you get to see the happiness it brings to the person who is helping you.

Exercise 26: Learning to Ask for Help

Think of a few things you can use help with, including childcare, carpooling, preparing healthy meals, grocery shopping, finding an exercise buddy or house or pet sitter. Think about what would free up some of your time and energy or help you pursue a goal easier. You can look at this as a one-time thing or set up something on a regular basis to help relieve stress. Whatever feels comfortable for you in this moment. Think about who you might ask. You might need to go to a local store or look in a local paper to find someone.

Take action. Send that email, make that call, or look up someone who can help. Get help for an area of your life where you feel you need it. If you can, think of other ways you might be able to lighten your load by incorporating the kindness and cooperation of others. Write down another action step you can take in the future to help yourself and allow someone else to help you simultaneously. You will be so grateful you did!

Whenever this help comes, notice how it feels and write about it. Think about other ways you might be able to ask for help in the future.

SELF-SABOTAGE

"The ego mind both professes its desire for love and does everything possible to repel it, or if it gets here anyway, to sabotage it. That is why dealing with issues like control, anger, and neediness is the most important work in preparing ourselves for love."

—MARIANNE WILLIAMSON

One might find it funny that this is the last chapter I wrote even though it is not the last chapter in the book. Even after years of studying and practicing personal development, the word "self-sabotage" still brings up an uncomfortable feeling. Why on Earth would anyone self-sabotage when we claim repeatedly we want to be happy? "That Darn Ego—Moving Past the Resistance to Change" in Section I explains part of the same reasoning. Even if we know changing our behaviors and patterns will make us feel better, help us achieve our goals, find a healthy relationship, and be in true happiness, there is this part of us still clinging to the old ways of our being. In noticing the self-sabotage, we can begin to come to some kind of peace with it, as we did with our shadows, and not let it rule us and totally throw us off balance.

We have heard of occurrences and seen this happen to people around us and ourselves, manifesting itself in many different ways. Perhaps you or a friend have consistently manifested unhealthy relationships even though the warning signs are always there. Maybe you know you want something so badly, whether it is losing that last ten pounds, writing that book, launching that business idea, exercising consistently, taking a class, or any other goal you may have, but something always seems to get in the way of completing that goal. The excuses keep on coming! You may have thought you were in the minority, but in fact, this is something that almost all of us in some way, shape, or form have and will consistently struggle with in different forms throughout our lives.

I have demonstrated in this book the many reasons why self-love and patience with oneself are so important. This is yet another case where it is crucial. When I recognized some of the ways I sabotaged myself (through busy-ing myself with non-crucial tasks) to avoid writing or almost being at my goal weight and then falling off track with exercise and healthy eating...I was pretty appalled. I teach this stuff for goodness sake, I need to live it. What on Earth was wrong with me? Saying those negative things to myself certainly made me pay attention to what was happening, but it did not motivate me. It made me want to throw up my hands in defeat and exclaim, "Okay, you win humanness, I guess my soul still hasn't figured this one out yet." But then I remembered that I had noticed my behavior and it was yet another old pattern that needed to be looked at. That darn pesky ego was at it again, telling me life was better and safer if I did not expand and change even as I claimed I was so ready to do. Better to be in my comfort zone and not risk the unknown. Well by now you know that is all total nonsense!

Think of someone in your life who seems to date the same exact person but yet complains about the same exact qualities each time. Perhaps you yourself have had some experience with this. You pick the same job, significant other, car, or service provider even though you know it is not in your best interest and will most likely cause you grief or anxiety—but for some reason you make excuses and repeat the same pattern. This is another reason self-love is so important. You need to love yourself in a few different ways when you deal with self-sabotage. You need to be kind and loving to yourself when you recognize that you are doing it. (Not an easy task and one where berating oneself comes easy!) You also need to love yourself enough to want to break this pattern, to know you are worthy of better, and to claim something different for yourself.

You can self-sabotage in so many ways and the easiest ones to notice are the ones that occur regularly: checking the Internet or your phone incessantly, which takes you away from the task at hand; watching too much television or binge watching movies or television shows online; making excuses to not do the things that you know are in your best interest; overeating if you are bored, sad, or worried even though you are concerned about your weight; holding emotions in so much that they begin to cause stress and physical ailments; saying you will commit to an exercise/spiritual/meditation regular practice but finding other distractions that keep you from beginning and maintaining it. The ways you can self-sabotage yourself are endless. But by figuring out your self-sabotaging behaviors, you can notice them and claim them, understanding this was the pattern up until this point. You can figure out a healthier pattern to take the place of the old one, and give yourself gratitude for noticing and encouragement to break this pattern even if it might take a little while.

There is the short-term self-sabotage and the longer-term self-sabotage such as picking the same relationship, job, etc., repeatedly that does not serve us. Noticing both will be of infinite use to you. I ask again that as these begin to surface and you acknowledge them, you give yourself a healthy dose of love. Know you are human and this is a common occurrence and one where you can break the pattern. I stress this self-love so much through this process because if our ego is pushed enough or if we are hard enough on ourselves, we can truly take ourselves into an even worse place and self-sabotage even worse than before. An example is someone who recognizes they overeat or eat unhealthy foods when they are upset. They notice this pattern and berate themselves for it or for their weight, thinking they should know better or be able to stop. But in berating themselves they throw themselves into even more of an emotional turmoil and trigger more emotional eating. Instead, by being kind and loving they can understand that this is a pattern that might repeat itself but they are cognizant of it and working on it. That deserves tons of credit and even if that person has an episode where that pattern reappears, they are aware of it now and maybe will only eat five cookies instead of ten or stop themselves in the middle of it. Any progress and even noticing after the fact deserves to be celebrated. You deserve gratitude to yourself for facing self-sabotage head on and knowing there is a possibility of real change!

Exercise 27: Breaking through Self-Sabotage

I want you to think of one of your self-sabotaging behaviors—one you do most often is best. Maybe you check your phone when you are with your friends or your children much more often than necessary instead of being present with them. Perhaps you have one of the behaviors mentioned in this chapter. If you get quiet for a few seconds and ask yourself, "What is a self-sabotaging behavior I have?," you will get an answer.

Look at this behavior and come up with another pattern you would like to put in its place. If it is emotional eating, perhaps it is to drink a cup of tea or water when you are in this state. If you have trouble committing to a spiritual practice daily, mark time on your calendar when you know you can have twenty minutes to yourself, even if it is just for one day this week for right now. Take this one step in knowing you can alter this pattern though it might take some work and some time.

Now, get into a quiet space as you are an expert at doing by now! Picture yourself when the triggering self-sabotaging behavior occurs and visualize yourself doing the new behavior. See how happy and proud you are of yourself when this new pattern is complete. Feel the unconditional love for yourself regardless.

Write down how you felt after that visualization. Commit to trying this new way of being instead of self-sabotaging the next times you see that behavior occurring. Commit to loving yourself throughout this process and showing yourself patience as you work on it. Whenever you do encounter this old/new paradigm, write about it; sit and think about it and give yourself gratitude and credit for committing to changing this old pattern that did not serve you.

INTENTION SETTING
Mini Goals

"Our intention creates our reality."
—DR. WAYNE DYER

We constantly send messages to the Universe with our thoughts and emotions. You have learned how to recognize old patterns of thoughts and ways to bring yourself to the present. Setting intentions is like placing an order with the Universe and deciding what you want to create. Since most of your time before now might have been spent worrying or saying what you don't want, it has allowed more of that to occur. With the tools you have now, tools that allow you to stay in the present moment and truly get to know the true you, you have likely unveiled new ways of thinking and new manifestations you want to bring into your life. Setting intentions and breaking them down into mini goals is a very powerful way to do just that!

When I went through the process of healing, I had no clue what would be next for me if I felt better. Many doctors had told me to expect to feel worse, to expect being on more and more painkillers, to expect a great deal of physical therapy in the future, and to expect to be confined to a wheelchair, possibly as soon as a year. I was so deeply in that space that the thoughts of what would be wonderful for me and what I wanted to create did not even enter my conscious mind. I would wake up and say things to myself such as, "I just want to get through the day." It was not a very lofty goal, but at the time it was all I could fathom. When I retrained my brain to pay gratitude and think positively, it soon became evident that I needed to start setting loftier goals.

I started simply with the goal of wanting to feel better. Physically, that was the only thing I could think of. A complete healing, by traditional Western doctors' prognoses, seemed to be completely out of the picture. But switching that little thought led to an opening of my mind, so I could set other goals. Well, what if I did feel even a little better? What then? By seeing it as a possibility, it sent more positive messages out to the Universe than "please let me get through the day without passing out in pain!" I broke down my life into parts and claimed to myself what I would love to manifest in every part of my life: physically, financially, emotionally, mentally, relationally, and spiritually. It became fun to fantasize about these scenarios, but I also noticed some resistance as I allowed myself to claim some of these lofty goals.

The resistance came from my ego, which is always good for stating what is right in front of us. My ego said, "But Jen, you are always in pain, how can you possibly expect to earn that much money?" It also asked, "But Jen, how can you think you will be able to exercise five times per week when you are in pain all the time?" A barrage of comments led me to recognize that maybe these big goals weren't enough. Maybe I needed to set some smaller attainable goals or create a first step for each goal, so my mind could adjust and I would not meet as much resistance. Hence, the mini goals.

Another reason for setting mini goals is to allow yourself time to adjust to those bigger goals. The world and everything in it is in a constant state of change. You might start off saying you want to lose twenty-five pounds, but as you get closer to that weight you realize that twenty is enough and you feel great! You might think you want a career in a certain field, but as you learn more about it, you are directed to a job you never even knew existed. By taking action, you allow more possibilities to open up. You can adjust the goals as you see and feel fit. No one else monitors them, judges them, or gives a commentary on them except for your own inner voice.

As you take steps toward any of your goals, it is important to congratulate yourself and give yourself credit! You know that if you were not doing something right, you would have a whole host of comments for yourself. Affirming that you are happy, that you are taking action, is another positive message you send to the Universe in claiming what you want. You have learned how powerful gratitude is. When gratitude is combined with self-love and action, life can change instantly.

Exercise 28: Setting Intentions with Mini Goals

Before you begin this exercise, put twenty minutes aside to write. Turn off your phone, use the restroom, turn on some quiet (instrumental) music, if you like, and settle in to a quiet spot. You may choose to do some breathing or some energy work to get yourself to a calm and centered space.

Set a goal in each of the following categories (Physical, Financial, Mental, Relational, Emotional, and Spiritual). Next, develop a first step or mini goal that you can attain in the near future. You can make a chart that looks like the following:

Area of Life	Goal	Mini Goal
Physical		
Financial		
Mental		
Relational		
Emotional		
Spiritual		

An example might be that you would love to think of yourself exercising (Physical) or Meditating (Spiritual) five to seven times a week. Let's say that right now you only do it once (if that much, in a week). It might be a big stretch for your mind to comprehend going from almost no practice or exercise to a near daily or daily practice. So your goal is what you see doing ideally and what you will strive toward, and your mini goal is what you can see as the first step toward that larger goal. If you do not exercise or meditate at all, once or twice per week, for fifteen minutes at a time might be a comfortable place to begin. The goal is to take that action step. Sometimes if you look at that big goal, you can become frozen in fear, meet resistance, and take no action. Mini goals allow for immediate action and results.

Look at this list and imagine for a few seconds each of these mini goals and goals as complete and see how that makes you feel. Write down the emotions that come up.

Take one step in one of these categories after you make this list. It can be any category but at least take one step toward achieving a mini goal. In doing so, you show the Universe you are taking action and are an active participant in making your dreams a reality. Please congratulate yourself on making the list and taking this step. Pay gratitude and know that by setting these intentions and goals, you have already taken the first step toward making them a reality.

EDUCATION

"Education is the key to unlock the golden door of freedom."
—GEORGE WASHINGTON CARVER

Educating yourself in something you are passionate about does not feel like effort at all. It feels joyful. It can sometimes feel like a "remembering," and it gets you so excited to learn more. Everyone has unique gifts and interests. Your passions and interests are part of what make you individual and so special in your own way. Educating yourself in something you are passionate about is the first step toward living the life of your dreams. It is time to pursue a passion, whether for work or your own personal satisfaction. Educating yourself in something that resonates with you will bring deep joy and fulfillment to your life.

I had always loved to dance. I began dance lessons at age six and studied until I was sixteen. Growing up in New York City allowed me the opportunity to dance in such places as Carnegie Hall and Lincoln Center. Dancing was always something that brought me joy and was something I felt passionate about. As a teenager, I decided it would be much more fun to go "clubbing" in New York City than to pursue formal dance. As an adult, I took various dance classes in hip hop, yoga dance, jazz, and salsa. Even when I was sick and in chronic pain, I went to yoga trance dance classes. Even on the days I was barely moving, it would bring me joy to be there. I was grateful for whatever I was able to do. I was devastated when the doctor told me I should not dance anymore because it would worsen my condition.

When I healed myself, I forgot about dance. I was so preoccupied with doing all the things I hadn't done for more than six years, that it didn't enter my mind to begin dancing again. Then one day I had lunch with two friends. My friend Amy asked my friend Swamiji, who always wears orange, "Why do you always wear orange?" He answered, "Because it is a simple thing I can do every day that brings me joy." He turned to me and asked, "What is something you can do every day that brings you joy?" Before I even had a chance to think about it, I blurted out, "Dance." I signed up for belly dancing lessons the very next day and was in a belly dance troupe for three years afterward.

We all have subjects that interest us, ideas that get us excited. We have heard about certain topics and said, "Wow, I would love to learn more about that." You can make up countless excuses not to pursue further education, even if it is something you are extremely interested in. You may say: "It costs too much," "I don't have the time," or "I'm too old to learn that." None of these are valid excuses. It is a case of the ego being comfortable and keeping you in the same place of non-change. When you follow an intuitive hit that said, "Wow, this looks like something I want to learn more about," it can change your life.

I would like to address some of the common excuses that come up around pursuing learning. The first is, "It costs too much." We are fortunate to live in a time when there are so many free resources to pursue learning. The Internet has a wealth of opportunities. I have had friends and clients learn different exercises, including, qi gong, yoga, and hula hooping via free online videos. Friends and clients have learned how to cook, sew, or craft by watching online videos and utilizing other free online resources. Many universities now offer free online courses. You can enter "Free Courses Online" in an online search, or go to a site such as www.coursera.org, which partners with more than eighty worldwide universities to offer free courses in every subject imaginable.

The second excuse is usually, "I don't have the time." Learning online also answers that complaint. When you learn on the Internet, you make the time whenever you can fit it in your schedule. Instead of watching television or doing something that numbs your mind, you can do something that enhances your brain functioning and brings you joy. It will be worth your time. If the Internet is not available, get a book from a local library or a bookstore and begin there. When you get excited about a topic or new ability, you will make the time to pursue it. You will probably shed some older habits that might not have served you and wasted a good deal of your time. You can learn a little bit at a time. I had a client who always felt a calling to learn about herbs but never had the time. This person found an online resource where they could learn at their own pace. Even if you invest five minutes in learning, it will be five minutes that excites you, and you will learn something new. Any time invested should be celebrated and is something to be grateful for.

The third excuse I hear most often is "I am too old to learn that." I have seen so many examples that indicate this simply is not true. Motivational author Louise Hay began taking Tango lessons in her seventies. I read an article about a woman who was ninety-eight and graduated from college for the first time. There is nothing you can't do if you are passionate about it. Your passion will drive you and allow you to make room for what you want to bring into your life.

When you resonate with something you want to learn, it truly is your soul speaking to you. Ignoring that voice can bring a sense of being unfulfilled or a feeling that you are missing out on an important part of your life. Pursuing that desire and seeing yourself get better at a hobby or talent, or learning more about a topic that interests you, will fill you with gratitude for yourself. It will give you a sense of accomplishment and might even jump-start a career path for you!

Exercise 29: Igniting Your Passions by Furthering Your Education

Think about a few things in your life that have interested you and that you have wanted to learn more about. Write them down, and put them in order from the thing that really gets you excited down to something that maybe you have a small curiosity about. Even if only one thing comes to mind, write it down.

Go online and look up whatever it is you are interested in, along with the words "free course." You can also look at online videos on sites such as YouTube. An example would be if you wanted to learn about cooking. Search online for "cooking free course," or go to YouTube and type in "cooking lessons." This can be done with any topic: meteorology, herbalism, foreign languages, drawing, energy work, dancing or any kind of exercise, science or history classes, and so much more. If you do not have Internet access, go to a library or bookstore and look up the topic. Borrow a book from the library or buy one book on the topic as a first action step. Even if you read a few pages a day, you gain knowledge on the topic.

If you have trouble coming up with one thing, take a break from thinking. Get quiet, sit with your hand on your heart, and ask yourself what is one subject you would like to learn more about and trust the answer will come.

Be kind to yourself during this process. When you find something, you might feel an urgency to learn it all at once. Remember, any step you take in this direction is more than you did yesterday and is worth giving yourself tons of gratitude for. There is no pressure except the pressure coming from you. Give yourself love and congratulations for taking this step in pursuing a passion!

PATIENCE WITH YOURSELF
AND OTHERS

"Be patient toward all that is unsolved in your heart and try to love the questions themselves ... Do not now seek the answers, which cannot be given to you because you would not be able to live them. And the point is to live everything. Live the questions."

—RAINER MARIA RILKE

Throughout these thirty exercises, you came across some aspects of yourself or patterns that you might have thought seemed less than favorable. Coming across these patterns, beliefs, or behaviors may have caused a whole range of emotions, including being upset, stressed, resistant, or sad. It is important to remember this is a process and some of these patterns and behaviors might have been in place for many years. Awareness, presence, and self-love are very important as you go through this process. Patience with yourself and others is of utmost importance too. There might be some growing pains. This is a natural part of healing. If you saw someone you loved going through pain you would comfort them and offer patience, do the same for yourself.

As you change, you will be more aware of the behaviors of others and your relationships to them as well as patterns you have in place within your relationships. I ask that you have patience with others as you are on this path of transformation. Know that we are not all in the same place on our journey. Others might react in a few different ways as they notice the transformation taking place in you. They might be curious and even excited for you, as they notice you are happier and making positive strides. Some might become aware that you are different and it might be a threat or scary to them as they don't fully understand what is happening; they just see something has changed.

In transforming yourself you raise your vibration to a higher level and as such other beliefs, old behaviors, and patterns that do not resonate at the new vibration will begin to feel "off." You might realize you don't feel called to be around some people you used to spend a significant amount of time with. You may have noticed as you went through "Influences" in Section I that it was not in your best interest to spend so much time with them. This does not make them "bad" people. We learn from every single person we encounter and what might have felt good or "right" for you in one stage of your life, may not feel okay anymore. Know this is okay.

If the people around you ask you what you have changed, share this book or other resources or tools you have used. The number one question I get from clients who have undergone serious shifts in perspective and being is, "What do I do if my significant other, family member, or good friend is not on the same page as me anymore?" Considering that in a loving relationship we want the best for each other, hopefully that person has noticed the positive changes in you and is supportive of them. Certainly share with that person whatever you are comfortable with if he or she is curious. If not, know that this might not be the right time for that person to start this journey and be patient. Going about your own work on yourself and making yourself the happiest person you can be is a great gift to a significant other and to everyone else around you as well as yourself.

Please keep in mind that even if you feel like you have "healed" a part of your life, that same exact pattern might sneak up again. I found this frustrating, and in the beginning when the same thing would pop up I would find myself self-deprecating and saying, "Didn't I go through this already?" Well, you might have but maybe you need to experience it from a different angle or in another way to fully get the lesson. Maybe it needs to be reaffirmed to prove to yourself that you are handling the situation differently. The best way I have found to deal with this is to pat myself on the back for even noticing I am in the pattern again. Before this awakening process, I would have just been "in it," letting my emotions get the best of me and not realizing I always had a choice in how to react. Being present offers you that choice! Being patient with yourself in this process allows you the freedom to know you might "take a (perceived) step back" once in a while. It is part of the learning process. One of the best parts about becoming present is this recognition of emotions and thoughts. Any hurdle or challenge you face can now be faced presently and, as such, will last much shorter than if you were to blindly follow your past patterns of behavior.

I ask that you remember this request for patience with yourself and others and offer exercises to come back to if you need a gentle reminder.

~~~~~~~~~~~~~~~~~~~~~~~~~~~

Exercise 30: Discovering Patience for Yourself and Others

Patience for Yourself

Take a few minutes and think about your biggest challenge as you went through this book and the exercises. Perhaps it was facing your shadows or self-sabotage. Maybe lightening up on the negative self-talk or achieving a state of self-love seems like it will be almost impossible to attain. Pick one of these that come to mind first and write it down in a positive statement:

I will show myself patience as I work toward achieving peace within myself, being present, and creating new patterns that serve my Highest Good while dealing with (and fill in whatever your biggest challenge is here).

Get quiet, bring in energy in your favorite way or watch your breathing, and get to a place of peace. Repeat the phrase that you have written down three times. As you do, imagine this challenge coming up in your life and visualize yourself being patient and showing yourself loving kindness when it comes up. Remember, even by noticing it you show so much more awareness of the situation than before and pay gratitude toward yourself for honoring this process.

Write down how you feel after you do this exercise. You can do this with as many challenges as you like.

Patience for Others

Think about someone who offers a challenge in patience for you. Specifically, if you can, someone who has come up as a challenge as you have begun to make these changes. Picture them in front of you and imagine they are happy for you and all the positive changes you have made. See them noticing, appreciating, and being thankful for you. Think of something you really treasure about this person and see yourself reflecting back your appreciation and patience with them. See yourself thanking them for their positive feedback and see them thanking you for your patience and love. Feel the gratitude between the two of you.

Please take some time to think about this and stay in that state of gratitude, love, and patience. Take a moment to write down what you felt.

SECTION IV
CONSIDERATIONS

This section offered you tools to stay on the path of transformation, aspects of yourself to notice, and ways to keep your growth unfolding. You will need to revisit these tools as you change and assess how they can be best utilized moving forward. Your goals in different areas of your life will change. As you notice and come to terms with some of your shadows, you will most likely reveal others that were more deeply hidden. What you need help with and who you will ask for help will change.

"The only thing constant in life is change," as Heraclitus said. The more you resist this change, the more you will be thrown around and feel like life is happening to you. The more you are conscious and present, loving to yourself and patient, the more life is in flow and you will ride those waves of change. Yes, you might get bumped around, but by using these tools and being cognizant that you are the Captain of the ship of your life you can truly steer yourself out of the most challenging of storms.

CONCLUSION

By this point you have experienced many changes, and I expect some were not so easy! I congratulate you on your dedication to do these exercises and thank you for taking the time to affirm to yourself that not only are you ready and willing to transform but also you are so worth it! Revisit these exercises and use these tools continuously in your life. You always grow, and there will be times when you experience setbacks. This is part of the growth process. Welcome it and know "this too shall pass." You have done tremendous work, and it has not gone unnoticed to your soul and to the people around you. Tell yourself you are willing to do this work and take continual action on it to create the life of your dreams and surpass the previous limitations you have held.

Remember to be present as often as possible and that each moment is a new one for you to create what you want and how you want your life to proceed. There is no "wrong" but there are easier roads to take. When you get quiet and present and listen to yourself rather than numbing out with past patterns, you can clearly see the next step on your path.

Love yourself, show yourself patience, and give yourself a ton of gratitude for being brave enough to stick with this journey and come to terms with some not so pleasant realizations, behaviors, and patterns. By recognizing them you are more than halfway there!

It has been a pleasure to present these words and exercises to aide you in your path of transformation. I wish you all the best as you continue your journey and am grateful for the opportunity to share a bit of my own with you.

BIBLIOGRAPHY

Books

Bengston, William, and Sylvia Fraser. *The Energy Cure*. Boulder, CO: Sounds True Inc., 2010.

Bolte-Taylor, Jill. *My Stroke of Insight*. New York: The Penguin Group, 2006.

Chopra, Deepak. *Perfect Health: The Complete Mind Body Guide*, revised and updated edition. New York: Three Rivers Publishing, 2001.

Dale, Cyndi. *The Complete Book of Chakra Healing: Activate the Transformative Power of Your Energy Centers*. Woodbury, MN: Llewellyn Publishing Worldwide, 2009.

————. *The Subtle Body: An Encyclopedia of Your Energetic Anatomy*. Boulder, CO: Sounds True Publishing, 2009.

Hall, Judy. *The Crystal Bible*. Cincinnati, OH: Walking Stick Press, 2003.

Minich, Deanna M. *Chakra Foods for Optimum Health: A Guide to the Foods That Can Improve Your Energy, Inspire Creative Changes, Open Your Heart, and Heal Body, Mind, and Spirit*. San Francisco, CA: Conari Press, 2009.

Myss, Caroline. *Anatomy of the Spirit*. New York: Harmony Books, 1996.

Vitale, Joseph, and Ihaleakala Hew Len. *Zero Limits: The Secret Hawaiian System for Wealth, Health, Peace, and More*. Hoboken, NJ: John Wiley & Sons, 2008.

Walsch, Neale Donald. *When Everything Changes, Change Everything: In a Time of Turmoil, a Pathway to Peace*. Ashland, OR: EmNin Books, 2009.

Internet Sources and Recommendations

Daily Good—News that Inspires: www.dailygood.org

Free Course Listings: www.coursera.org

Huffington Post (Good News): www.huffingtonpost.com /good-news

Jill Bolte Taylor – TED Talk: www.ted.com/talks/jill_bolte _taylor_s_powerful_stroke_of_insight?language=en

New Earth Daily: newearthdaily.com

Positive News: www.positivenewsus.org

Shaman Lench Archuletta: windspiritteaching.com

Silva Life System: www.silvalifesystem.com

Steve G. Jones, Hypnotherapist: www.stevegjones.com

Sunny Skyz: http://www.sunnyskyz.com/good-news

The Happy News: www.thehappynews.com

Articles

Gabriel, Roger. "How to use Sound to Heal Yourself." www.chopra
.com/ccl/how-to-use-sound-to-heal-yourself

Goldman, Jonathan. "Sound and the Chakras." www.healingsounds
.com/sound-and-the-chakras

"Poses for the Chakras." www.yogajournal.com/category/poses
/anatomy/chakra-opening/

Walsh, Sarah. "7 Yoga Poses to Balance Your Chakras." www
.mindbodygreen.com/0-11865/7-yoga-poses-to-balance-your-
chakras.html

To Write to the Author

If you wish to contact the author or would like more information about this book, please write to the author in care of Llewellyn Worldwide Ltd. and we will forward your request. Both the author and publisher appreciate hearing from you and learning of your enjoyment of this book and how it has helped you. Llewellyn Worldwide Ltd. cannot guarantee that every letter written to the author can be answered, but all will be forwarded. Please write to:

Jenny Mannion
℅ Llewellyn Worldwide
2143 Wooddale Drive
Woodbury, MN 55125-2989

Please enclose a self-addressed stamped envelope for reply, or $1.00 to cover costs. If outside the U.S.A., enclose an international postal reply coupon.

Many of Llewellyn's authors have websites with additional information and resources. For more information, please visit our website at http://www.llewellyn.com.